THE WISDOM OF LAO TZU

PRONUNCIATION OF CHINESE NAMES

In English. It is made with difficulty by Westerners, but is actually the vowel sound produced when the sound of *z* is prolonged and definitely vocalised ('buzzing' sound). In this instance, I depart from the Wade system, which renders it as *tzu*, because of its cumbersomeness. It frequently appear in names like *Lao tzu, Chuang tzu, T'sengtse, Tsesze.*

The vowel sound indicated by the combination *ih* does not exist in English. It is made when the tongue and lip positions of the English *sh* are held unchanged and vocalised. For practical purposes, read the *ih* as *ee* (or if possible as a sound in between *she* and *shir*); there's no use trying to reproduce the sound exactly.

The important diphthongs are: *ia, ai, ou, uo, ei, ieh, ua*-all pronounced with their individual approximate Latin values(*h* in *ieh* is not pronounced).
ao may be pronounced nearly as *aw*.

Combinations like *in, ing, an, ang* are pronounced with the usual Latin values for the sounds *(in, ing, ahn, ahng)*. But *en, eng* are pronounced as *ern, erng*, or for practical purposes as *un, ung (sun, sung)* in English, whereas Chinese *un, ung* must be pronounced as *oon, oong.*

The distinction between *sh* and *hs* is a nuisance for English readers: read both as *sh* for practical purposes. Technically, the sound *hs* is different and comes invariably before *i* and *u*. Since the two groups are clearly separated by the occurrence or absence of a following *i* or *u*, that distinction in spelling between *sh* and *hs* is totally unnecessary for Chinese readers, and meaningless for Westerners.

The Chinese language distinctly differentiates between aspirated and unaspirated *p, t, k, ch, ts*. For practical purposes read *p, t, k, ch, ts* as *b, d, g, j, dz*, and read *p', t', k', ch', ts'* like the regular English *p, t, k, ch, ts*.

Remember therefore to follow the Latin values for the vowels as a general principle, and for practical purposes read:
hs as *sh*
ih as *ee* (or *ir*)
ieh as *y-ay*
eh as *er*
en as *un*
eng as *ung*

CONTENTS

INTRODUCTION

PROLEGOMENA

BOOK OF TAO
(*The chapter headings indicate the text of Lao tzu; section headings indicate selections from Chuang tzu.*)

Book I.
THE CHARACTER OF TAO
1. ON THE ABSOLUTE TAO
   1. The Tao that cannot be named, told, or discussed.
   2. The conditioned and the unconditioned.
   3. All things are One. The eye of the senses and the eye of the spirit.
   4. The gate to the secret of all life.
2. THE RISE OF RELATIVE OPPOSITES
   1. The relativity of opposites. The levelling of all things and attributes into One.
   2. The relativity of all standards. Dependence on subjective viewpoint.
   3. The futility of language. On preaching the doctrine without words.
   4. The futility of argument.
3. ACTION WITHOUT DEEDS
   1. Exalt not the wise. A world of unconscious goodness.
   2. Knowledge is the instrument of contention.
   3. How the increase of knowledge and the teachings of philosophers corrupted the nature of man.
   4. The doctrine of inaction (*laissez-faire, non-interference*), seen as a teaching to allow the people to 'fulfil peacefully the natural instincts of life.'

4. THE CHARACTER OF TAO
   1. Tao is like the sea.
5. NATURE
   1. Nature is unkind. The Sage is unkind.
   2. Tao is like a bellows.
6. THE SPIRIT OF THE VALLEY
   1. The silent beautiful universe. The 'root' of all things.

Book II.
THE LESSONS OF TAO

7. LIVING FOR OTHERS
   1. The impartiality of Tao. Another reason for inaction.
   2. Heaven covers all equally.
   3. The Sage is impartial.
8. WATER
   1. Water as the symbol of heavenly virtue.
   2. The Tao of God and the Tao of man.
9. THE DANGER OF OVERWEENING SUCCESS
   1. The smugs, the snugs and the hump-back.
   2.-3. The dangers of hoarding wealth.
   4. Inscription on humility.
   5. The story of butcher Yueh.
10. EMBRACING THE ONE
    1. Lao tzu on mental hygiene.
    2. The sons of Heaven and the sons of men.
11. THE UTILITY OF NOT-BEING
    1. The usefulness of not-being
    2. The use of uselessness.
    3. The comfort of unawareness.
12. THE SENSES
    1. The five senses detract from our nature.
    2. Action of the wind on water.
    3. Distractions of the material world.
13. PRAISE AND BLAME
    1. Definition of honour and happiness.
    2. Ownership.
    3. The perfect man is selfless.

4. 'Entrusting that which belongs to the universe to the whole universe.'

Book III.
THE IMITATION OF TAO
14. PREHISTORIC ORIGINS
  1.-2.-3. The invisible, inaudible and intangible.
  4. The parable of the animals, the wind and the mind.

15. THE WISE ONES OF OLD
  1. The demeanour of the pure man.
  2. Confucius on water.

16. KNOWING THE ETERNAL LAW
  1. The Sage uses his mind like a mirror.
  2. Calm as a counter-agent against nervousness.
  3. 'Returning to the Root.' Conversation between General Clouds and the Great Nebulous.
  4. The origin of things and reversion to the grand harmony.

17. RULERS
  1. Emperor Yao's teacher.
  2. Emperor Yao's reign.
  3. How man's character declined.
  4. Conversation between Lao tzu and Yangtse on the best ruler.

18. THE DECLINE OF TAO
  1. On the decline of the great Tao, the doctrine of 'humanity' and 'justice' arose.
  2. The origin of hypocrisy.

19. REALISE THE SIMPLE SELF
  1. 'Opening Trunks.'
  2. 'Be careful not to interfere with the natural goodness of the heart of man.'

20. THE WORLD AND I
  1. The demeanour of the man of character.
  2. The common herd of men.

21. MANIFESTATIONS OF TAO
  1. Through inaction the heaven becomes clear.

2. The life-force of perfect Tao.
    3. The character of Tao.
22. FUTILITY OF CONTENTION.
    1. The utility of futility.
    2. Hunchback Su. The virtue of deformities.
    3. Two useless trees.
    4. The acceptance of conventions.
23. IDENTIFICATION WITH TAO
    1. Description of a storm. Music of the earth.
24. THE DREGS AND TUMOURS OF VIRTUE.
    1. Advice against ostentation.
    2. Two barmaids.
    3. 'He who reveals himself is not luminous.' The definition of 'good.'
    4. 'He who boasts of himself is not given credit.'
25. THE FOUR ETERNAL MODELS
    1. The mystery of the universe.
    2. Tao is named 'Great.' The eternal cycles.
    3. Complete, Entire and All.

Book IV.
THE SOURCE OF POWER
26. HEAVINESS AND LIGHTNESS
    1. No heed to worldly affairs.
    2. On letting one's self run away with desires of the body.
27. ON STEALING THE LIGHT
    1. The Sage rejects no person.
28. KEEPING TO THE FEMALE
    1. The horse-trainer Polo.
    2. On returning to nature.
29. WARNING AGAINST INTERFERENCE
    1. To have territory is to have something great.
    2. Anecdote about Confucius.
30. WARNING AGAINST THE USE OF FORCE
    1. The danger of relying on an army.
31. WEAPONS OF EVIL
    1. On the emptiness of victory.

    2. The dilemma of war and peace.
32. TAO IS LIKE THE SEA
    1. Seek repose in what the human mind cannot know.
    2. 'Knowing where to stop.' Chuang tzu's sayings on the unknowable.
33. KNOWING ONESELF
    1. On wealth and poverty.
    2. The skull.
    3. Chuang tzu's wife died.
    4. Chuang tzu was about to die.
    5. Lao tzu died.
    6. The conversation of four friends on life and death.
    7. The conversation of three friends on life and death.
34. THE GREAT TAO FLOWS EVERYWHERE
    1. The immanence of Tao.
    2. Tao is everywhere.
35. THE PEACE OF TAO
    1. Peace through holding the Tao.
    2. Temper knowledge with mildness.
    3. "Applied, its supply never fails."
36. THE RHYTHM OF LIFE
    1. The doctrine of reversion.
    2. To be united is to be parted.
    3. Signs of failure and success.
37. WORLD PEACE
    1. The doctrine of inaction and quietude.
    2. 'The world arrives at peace of its own accord.' The imitation of nature.
38. DEGENERATION
    1. The decline of Tao.
    2. The proper place of human institutions.
    3. How Confucian doctrines lead to chaos.
    4. Unconscious goodness.
39. UNITY THROUGH COMPLEMENTS.
    1. The power of Tao.
    2. The power behind spring and autumn.
    3. How a sage lives in the world.
40. THE PRINCIPLE OF REVERSION

1. Reversion is the action of Tao.
2. The origin of things. Evolution of being from not-being.

Book V.
THE CONDUCT OF LIFE
41. QUALITIES OF THE TAOIST
   1. "Sheer white appears like tarnished; great character appears like insufficient."
42. THE VIOLENT MAN
   1. 'Out of Tao, One is born.'
43. THE SOFTEST SUBSTANCE
   1. 'That-which-is-without-form penetrates that-which has-no-crevice.' The parable of the butcher.
44. BE CONTENT
   1. Chuang tzu was in a park.
   2. On losing one's real life.
   3. Confucius received advice from a Taoist.
   4. Those who understand life.
   5. Chuang tzu refused government office.
45. CALM QUIETUDE
46. RACING HORSES
   1. The Tit
47. PURSUIT OF KNOWLEDGE
   1. Confucius on the 'fasting of the heart.'
48. CONQUERING THE WORLD BY INACTION
49. THE PEOPLE'S HEARTS
   1. 'The Sage regards the people's opinions and feelings as his own.'
   2. Following the people.
50. THE PRESERVING OF LIFE
   1. Life is the companion of death, and death is the beginning of life.
   2. The agitations of man's soul.
   3. Those who dream of the banquet wake up to lamentation and sorrow.
   4. Human life is short.
   5. Mengsun's death. The self may be a dream.

    6. Chuang tzu dreaming of being a butterfly.
    7. Kuangch'engtse on becoming an immortal.
    8. Why the man of Tao is beyond all harm.
51. THE MYSTIC VIRTUE
52. STEALING THE ABSOLUTE
    1. On knowing and not knowing the Oneness of things.
    2. Tao unifies the parts.
    3. The Sage rests in the solution of things.
53. BRIGANDAGE
    1. Think for the pigs.
    2. On true happiness.
54. THE INDIVIDUAL AND THE STATE
    1. The nine tests of Confucius for judging men.
55. THE CHARACTER OF THE CHILD
    1. Wholeness of talent: Ugly T'o.
    2. Wholeness of character: The fighting cock.
    3. The new-born calf; the art of concentration.
    4. The shadow, the body and the spirit.
    5. On 'Not improving upon life.'
56. BEYOND HONOUR AND DISGRACE
    1. 'He who knows does not speak; he who speaks does not know.'
    2. It is difficult not to talk about Tao.
    3. The relativity of knowledge.
    4. The mystic virtue.
    5. 'Love and hatred cannot touch him; profit and loss cannot reach him.'

Book VI.
THE THEORY OF GOVERNMENT

57. THE ART OF GOVERNMENT
    1. The bad influence of machines.
    2. Why there are criminals.
58. LAZY GOVERNMENT
59. BE SPARING
    1. 'The art of nourishing the spirit.'
    2. Perfect talent.

    3. See the Solitary One.
    4. Getting rid of mind and body.
60. RULING A BIG COUNTRY
    1. The Sage does no harm to the people.
    2. The spirits cease to do people harm
61. BIG AND SMALL COUNTRIES
62. THE GOOD MAN'S TREASURE
    1. Why reject people?
63. DIFFICULT AND EASY
    1. Requite evil with virtue.
64. BEGINNING AND END
    1. 'Be careful at the end as at the beginning.'
    2. Learning what the multitude have lost.
65. THE GRAND HARMONY
    1. The origin of world chaos.
    2. The harm done to man's nature by the 'sages.'
    3. Prediction of cannibalism. The futility of the Confucian solution.
    4. Going back to nature. Parable of the sea bird.
66. THE LORDS OF THE RAVINES
    1. Being like an inferior to people.
67. THE THREE TREASURES
68. THE VIRTUE OF NOT-CONTENDING
    1. On not fighting.
69. CAMOUFLAGE
70. THEY KNOW ME NOT
71. SICK-MINDEDNESS
72. ON PUNISHMENT (1)
73. ON PUNISHMENT (2)
74. ON PUNISHMENT (3)
75. ON PUNISHMENT (4)
    1. On valuing life.

Book VII.
APHORISMS

76. HARD AND SOFT
77. BENDING THE BOW

   1. To have enough is good luck.
78. NOTHING WEAKER THAN WATER
   1. On weakness overcoming strength.
79. PEACE SETTLEMENTS
   1. On the futility of treaties.
80. THE SMALL UTOPIA
   1. The Age of Perfect Character.
81. THE WAY OF HEAVEN
   1. True words are not fine-sounding.
   2. He gives to other people.
   3. Where can I find a man who forgets about words?
IMAGINARY CONVERSATIONS BETWEEN LAO TZU AND CONFUCIUS

Introduction

WHILE Confucius is more popularly known to the average man in the West, a small group of critics and scholars in this country, for some years now, have been strong admirers of Lao tzu and his extraordinary little volume. In fact, I may venture the opinion that among scholars who know the Orient, there are more devotees of Lao tzu than of Confucius, and the case is rare when a discerning reader does not fall under the affable charm of the book. Probably because of its small size, the Book of Tao is also the most translated of all Chinese texts, there being twelve translations in English and nine in German. For while good sense belongs to Confucius, wit and depth and brilliance belong to the Taoist sage, whose name has been aptly and affectionately translated as the 'Old Boy.' This impression of Western readers is borne out by that of Chinese of ancient times before Confucianism became more or less established by Emperor Han Wuti as the orthodox faith in 136 B.C. 'Huan T'an says, "Lao Tan (**Lao tzu** or **Laotse**) wrote two chapters discussing Nothingness, deprecating humanity and justice and criticizing the study of li (Confucianism), but his admirers seem to think them even better than the Five Classics. Both Emperors Wen and Ching (179-143B.C.) and Szema Ch'ien (145-after 85 B.C.)expressed this opinion."

After 136 B.C., a sharp division was made. Officials liked Confucius and writers and poets liked Chuang tzu and Lao tzu, and when the writers and poets became officials, they liked Confucius openly and Lao tzu and Chuang tzu secretly.[1]

1. There were exceptions. There were periods in Chinese history when Taoism took a dominant position among the literati and became almost a cult, as in the third and fourth centuries A.D., or when it was officially encouraged by the Emperor himself, as in the T'ang Dynasty (eighth to tenth centuries). I was touched, however, to see that Wang Hsien-ch'ien, the man who spent his lifetime to produce the best and standard edition of Chuang tzu with commentaries, tried to minimise his own work by deprecating Chuang tzu in his preface as late as 1908. The same is true of Wei Yuan's commentaries on Lao tzu. Lip service was always given Confucianism as a better doctrine, and appreciation of the beauty of Chuang tzu was always sly and restrained.

It must also be admitted at the outset that if any Chinese sage was distinguished for talking in proverbs, it was Lao tzu and not Confucius. Somehow Lao tzu's aphorisms communicate an excitement which Confucian humdrum good sense cannot. Confucian philosophy is a philosophy of social order, and order is seldom exciting; it deals with human relationships, and preoccupation with human relationships of the workaday world is apt to dull one's senses to the spiritual yearnings and imaginative fights of which the human soul is capable. Confucians worship culture and reason; Taoists reject them in favour of nature and intuition, and the one who rejects anything always seems to stand on a higher level and therefore always seems more attractive than the one who accepts it. Confucius was a positivist; Lao tzu a mystic. After a man has been a dutiful man and a good father and a good provider for the family, what about the mystery and beauty of the universe, the meaning of life and death, the quakings of the inner soul and that sad feeling of the wistful-minded that beyond the world of positive knowledge there is a realm of forces unseen, which we can feel but can never know?

The first reaction of anyone scanning the *Book of Tao* is laughter; the second reaction, laughter at one's own laughter; and the third, a feeling that this sort of teaching is very much needed today. Lao tzu says:

When the highest type of men hear the Tao (truth)
They try hard to live in accordance with it.

When the mediocre hear the Tao,
They seem to be aware and yet unaware of it.
When the lowest type hear of Tao ,
They break into loud laughter.
If it were not laughed at, it would not be Tao.

I am quite sure that the reaction of the majority of readers on first looking into Lao tzu's book will be to laugh. I say this without any disrespect, for I did that myself. The highest type of scholars end by laughing with Lao tzu at the preoccupations of the philosophers of the day. After that, Lao tzu becomes a lifelong friend.

Lao tzu says, 'In my words, there is a principle. In the affairs of men, there is a system. Because they know not these, they also know me not.' Lao tzu's philosophy of life and the universe as revealed in his separate witticisms and the unconscious assumptions and relationships of its tenets should be made plain to the reader. Lao tzu's epigrams are flashes of insight, like some of the best intuitive passages of Emerson, but the epigrams of both can be better understood through an understanding of the transcendentalism of Emerson and Lao tzu. His epigrammatic flashes are like perfectly cut gems: they stand complete in themselves and often shine better without embellishments. But the mind of man ever craves for comprehension on a higher level. Moreover, Lao tzu's gems of oracular wisdom lend themselves to diversified interpretations, even in Chinese-much more so in the words of a translator into English where the two languages are so radically different in concepts. The correct approach would be to read them along with interpretations by ancient Chinese Taoist scholars, like Han Fei and Huainantse who lived a few centuries after him. Han Fei (?-234 B.C.) wrote two chapters in his works devoted exclusively to interpretations of passages of Lao tzu, especially from the latter part of the book, which deals with the practical applications in life and government rather than with the principles of Taoist philosophy. Huainantse (Liu An, about 178-122 B.C.) also elucidated a great number of passages, and the works of Liehtse and Wentse also contain relevant passages. The best approach, however, would be to read Lao tzu with Chuang tzu. After all, Chuang tzu was his greatest disciple and the greatest exponent of Taoism. He was closer to Lao tzu in time than Han Fei and helped to shape the development of Taoist thought. As the viewpoint of the two philosophers was almost identical, it would be easy to cull passages from the more than one hundred thousand words of Chuang tzu and arrange them in order to illustrate Lao tzu's meaning, something which has never been done before.

In the centuries before Christ, Taoism was known as 'The science of the Yellow Emperor and Lao tzu.' Then there came a change. Chuang tzu's popularity steadily rose and his name was ranked with that of Lao tzu and identified with Taoist thought. In the later Han and Chin dynasties (roughly the first four centuries A.D.), Taoism ceased to be known as the science of the Yellow Emperor and Lao tzu, but was spoken of as the philosophy of 'Lao and Chuang.' And one should not wonder, for one of the reasons for the popularity of Taoist literature with the scholars was the charm of Chuang tzu's prose. By all standards of charm of style and depth of thought, Chuang tzu was, in my opinion, the greatest prose master in the classical period. Chuang tzu had the grand manner: his language was crisp and firm, but his style was fluid, often personal; his thoughts were profound, but his presentation was light and whimsical. Even his faults were those of a humorist and a writer who had too much to say, whose imagery and metaphors came sometimes a little too readily. As I went over the work of Chuang tzu several times in the course of compilation of the present volume, I noticed that more phrases coined by Chuang tzu have passed into the phraseology of literature as strictly literary expressions than were derived even from Confucius' Analects.

The fundamental basis of thinking and the character of ideas of the two philosophers were the same. But while Lao tzu spoke in aphorisms, Chuang tzu wrote long, discursive philosophical essays. While Lao tzu was all intuition, Chuang tzu was all intellect. Lao tzu smiled; Chuang tzu laughed. Lao tzu taught; Chuang tzu scoffed. Lao tzu spoke to the heart; Chuang tzu spoke to the mind. Lao tzu was like Whitman, with the large and generous humanity of Whitman; Chuang tzu was like Thoreau, with the ruggedness and hardness and impatience of an individualist. To go back to the period of the Enlightenment, Lao tzu was like Rousseau in his harking back to nature; Chuang tzu was like Voltaire in the sharpness of his sting. Chuang tzu wrote of himself, 'With unbridled fancies, facetious language and sweet romantic nonsense, he gives free play to his spirit without restraint.' It must be admitted that Chuang tzu was often playful and facetious. Incidentally, Westerners need not criticize Confucius: Chuang tzu bit him hard enough. This is an aspect in Chuang tzu as a writer which often displeased the orthodox mandarins; but a nihilist who saw through the folly and futility of the Confucian saviours of the world should be allowed some fun. It would be unfair to expect him always to wear a despondent countenance over the failure of the Confucians.

Of Lao tzu we know very little except the bare facts that he was born in K'uhsien in 571 B.C.; that he was a contemporary of Confucius, probably twenty years older; that he came from an old, cultured family and was a Keeper of the Imperial Archives at the capital; that he retired and disappeared in middle life and lived probably to a grand old age, possibly over ninety, not over one hundred and sixty as Szema Ch'ien says, and left a long progeny of grandchildren, one of whom became an official.

As in the case of Jesus, a few scholars doubted that Lao tzu ever lived, or that his work was his own. As a matter of fact, several works of the third century B.C., besides Chuang tzu's, mentioned Lao tzu and gave quotations from the *Book of Tao*. It should be remembered that critical scepticism became almost a disease in the Manchu Dynasty, and in the case of Lao tzu this may be attributed to the pernicious influence of Liang Ch'i-ch'ao, who thought that Lao tzu's book was most probably produced by some forgers in the third century. There was so much loose talk about forgery, and textual critics could not distinguish between a forged work and later interpolations of single passages. Therefore, when one hears a Chinese scholar saying that Lao tzu, or the great majority of the chapters of Chuang tzu, was a forgery, without sufficient show of evidence or exact reasoning, one may be sure that he is merely aping a fashion which has by now become very tiresome.

Chuang tzu died about 275 B.C., at what age it is not clear. He was thus a contemporary of Mencius, and a close friend of Huei Shih. A native of Mengshien, his only known position was that of an 'Officer of the Varnish Grove' there. He was married, and was not known to have any children. To the popular imagination of the Chinese people, Chuang tzu is known as the man who sat on the ground and sang, beating time on a basin, while his wife's coffin was lying in a corner of the house awaiting burial. And yet one of the world's most profound statements on life and death were expressed when his disciples questioned him on his peculiar conduct.

Probably the wittiest saying of Chuang tzu was a joke about his own death. It is a joke with a poet's touch." Another favourite anecdote of his was typical of his style. Once Chuang tzu dream he was a butterfly and while he was in that dream, he fluttered among the flowers and was quite sure he was a butterfly. When he awoke, he said to himself, 'Now am I Chuang Chou dreaming of being a butterfly, or a butterfly dreaming of being Chuang Chou?' But his sharpest shafts were always directed at official pomp and dignity; and then Chuang tzu could be mean and caustic. A poor scholar of Sung once went to see the king and returned in glory, with a number of carriages and a retinue presented to him by the king. The scholar was very proud of the success of his visit, and Chuang tzu said to him, 'There was once a king of Ch'in who was ill. He gave one carriage to a physician who lanced his tumour, but five carriages to one who cured his pile. The lower down you go, the richer the reward. Did you cure the king's pile?'

This character of Chuang tzu enables us to see some of the differences between the two Taoist sages. In the preparation of this book I made a concordance of the ideas of Lao tzu and Chuang tzu for my own purposes. I discovered that the character of their teachings was almost identical, but I also found two important differences. First, the principal teaching of Lao tzu is humility. His recurrent theme, on which he spoke more than on any other single subject, was gentleness, resignation, the futility of contentions ('Never be the first of the world'), the strength of weakness and the tactical advantage of lying low It is difficult, if not impossible, to find parallel sayings of Chuang tzu on the subject. To be sure, starting from the same basic philosophy, Chuang tzu had to believe in humility, but he never could quite say it. Where Lao tzu spoke of the virtue of non-contention, Chuang tzu was inclined to speak of the virtue of quiescence, of keeping and preserving one's spiritual power through tranquility and rest. To Lao tzu, water is the 'softest of all substances' and a symbol of the wisdom of seeking lowly places,' but to Chuang tzu it is a symbol of tranquility of the mind and clarity of spirit, and of enormous reserve power in inaction. While Lao tzu urged the importance of failure, or at least of appearing to fail (for Lao tzu was the first philosopher of camouflage), Chuang tzu scoffed at the glitter of success. Lao tzu praised the humble; Chuang tzu lambasted the great. While Lao tzu preached contentment, Chuang tzu's most characteristic teaching was to let man's spirit 'roam in the metaphysical sphere,' the sphere above physical things. And while Lao tzu frequently mentioned the strength of 'the female' in 'overcoming the male, Chuang tzu remained a man's man and had nothing to say on the subject.

The second difference is: Chuang tzu not only developed a complete theory of knowledge and reality and the futility of language, but felt and expressed more poignantly the pathos of human life. What was philosophy in Lao tzu became poetry in Chuang tzu. With all the consolation of philosophy, Chuang tzu felt the pang and sorrow of man's short life, and certainly his most beautiful passages are on the subject of life and death. 'Those who dream of the banquet wake to lamentation and sorrow. Those who dream of lamentation and sorrow wake to join the hunt.' 'What we love is the mystery of life. What we hate is corruption in death. But the corruptible in its turn becomes mysterious life, and this mysterious life once more becomes corruptible.' Personally, I regard the passage on 'Agitations of the Soul' as the finest writing by Chuang tzu, or by any Chinese writer of ancient times.

II

Lao tzu is full of paradoxes. They became almost a mannerism with him. 'Do nothing and everything is done.' 'Because the sage is able to forget his self, therefore his self is realized.' The making of a paradox is like the formation of a crystal. A crystal is formed when a certain material is subjected to a certain change of temperature, and when that condition obtains, not one crystal, but a great number of them, are formed at the same time. A paradoxical statement is made when one takes a basic point of view or a scale of values which is diametrically opposite to the one commonly accepted. Jesus's paradox, 'He who loses life shall find it, starts from n the conception of two distinct levels of life, the spiritual and the physical; but putting the two together, one obtains what appears on the surface to be a paradoxical saying.

What is the basic point of view of Lao tzu which is so productive of paradoxes and which makes it possible for him to teach the strength of weakness, the advantage of lying low, the warning against overweening success? The answer is to be found in the doctrine of universal reversion, of eternal cycles of every end becoming a beginning, and things reverting to their original state. Since life is a constant flux and change, rise and decay alternate like day and night, and reaching the prime of one's strength marks the beginning of decline.

Lao tzu said, 'It (the origin of the universe) is a problem that defies the mind and language of man. I will try to tell you what it is like approximately. The great *yin* is majestically silent; the great *yang* is impressively active. Majestic silence comes from heaven, and impressive activity comes from the earth. When the two meet and merge, all things are formed. Some can see the connection but cannot see their form. Growth alternates with decay, fullness with exhaustion, darkness with light. Everyday things change, and every month they are transformed. You see what is going on every day and observe that the change is imperceptible. Life comes from a source and death is but return to it. Thus beginning follows the end in a continua endless cycle. Without Tao, what can be the generative principle binding on all?'

Probably the best approach to Lao tzu's philosophy is through Emerson in his important essay on 'Circles,' which is fundamentally Taoist. Emerson uses the apostrophe, 'O circular philosopher.' From the philosophy of circles,' Emerson derives exactly the same consequences as Lao tzu. Emerson taught that' every end is a beginning; that there is always another dawn risen on mid-noon, and under every deep a lower deep opens.'Huei Shih taught, "When the sun is at its zenith, it is setting somewhere else, and Chuang tzu wrote, 'To Tao, the zenith is not high, nor the nadir low.' Emerson taught, 'There are no fixtures in nature': 'There are no fixtures to men.' Consequently, 'The new continents are built out of the ruins of the old planet the new races fed out of the decomposition of the foregoing.' From the circular philosophy, Emerson produced Lao tzu an paradoxes. 'The highest prudence is the lowest prudence,' 'The virtues of society are the vices of the saint,' People wish to be settled; only as far as they are unsettled, is there any hope for them.' For the above Emersonian paradoxes, the reader will be able to find exact, and sometimes verbal, parallels in the selections from Chuang tzu. Emerson's two essays, 'Circles' and "The Over-soul, are completely Taoist, and one appreciates them better after reading Lao tzu. He also reached the same belief regarding the relativity of opposites: 'One man's beauty is another's ugliness; one man's wisdom, another's folly.' And Emerson quoted some Yankee farmer speaking a typical Taoist proverb: 'Blessed be nothing. The worse things are, the better they are.'

as a philosophy, therefore, may be summed up as follows: It is a philosophy of the essential unity of the universe(monism), of reversion, polarisation (*yin* and *yang*), and eternal cycles, of the levelling of all differences, the relativity of all standards, and the return of all to the Primeval One, the divine intelligence, the source of all things. From this naturally arises the absence of desire for strife and contention and fighting for advantage. Thus the teachings of humility and meekness of the Christian Sermon on the Mount find a rational basis and a peaceable temper is bred in man. In his emphasis on nonresistance to evil, Lao tzu became the precursor to a long line of thinkers and moralists culminating in Tolstoy as the greatest modern disciple of Christian humility and forbearance. It were well that some of the world leaders (are there any?) would read Lao tzu's saying on war (Ch. 30-31, selection 68.I), military tactics (Ch. 68-69), peace settlements (Ch. 79) and disarmament (selection 31.1). It would have been better still if Hitler had had a little of the subtlety of Lao tzu,
'Stretch a bow to the very full.
And you will wish you had stopped in time,'
before the Nazi bow snapped. We might have been spared much bloodshed.

III

If compelled to indicate my religion on an immigration blank, I might be tempted to put down the word 'Taoist,' to the amazement of the customs officer who probably never heard of it. The thought has been constantly on my mind to find a religion that is acceptable to a scientist. For this is the central problem of the age. The Tao of the Taoist is the divine intelligence of the universe, the source of things, the life-giving principle; it informs and transforms all things; it is impersonal. impartial, and has little regard for individuals. It is immanent formless, invisible, and eternal. Best of all, the Taoist does not presume to tell us about God; he insists to the point of repetitiousness that Tao cannot be named and the Tao which is named is not Tao. Above all, the one important message of Taoism is the oneness and spirituality of the material universe.

I have been watching the progress of scientific thought, and have reason to believe that the period of crass materialism of the nineteenth century is fast tottering, because it is no longer tenable in the light of modern physics. While Karl Marx was developing his materialistic dialectic in the flush of mechanistic science, a New England sage wrote, uncannily:
'Fear not the new generalisation. Does the fact look crass and material, threatening to degrade thy theory of spirit? Resist it not; it goes to refine and raise thy theory of matter just as much.'

This was published in 1847. Meanwhile, the physicists have been digging from under the foundations of matter itself. As Eddington summarises the century of research, We have chased the solid substance from the continuous liquid to the atom, from the atom to the electron, and there we have lost it.'1sWhat the electron is doing inside the atom is summarised in the following line, '*Something unknown is doing we don't know what.*' Somewhere in the quantum of light, the corpuscular and the non-corpuscular meet and confuse and exasperate the investigator of truth. A century has passed now since Emerson wrote, and a cycle has been completed. Eddington wrote:

'It will perhaps be said that the conclusion to be drawn from these arguments from modern science is that religion first became possible for a reasonable scientific man about the year 1927. If we must consider that tiresome person, the consistently reasonable man, we may point out that not merely religion, but most of the ordinary aspects of life first became possible for him in that year. Certain common activities (e.g. falling in love) are, I fancy, still forbidden him. If our expectation should prove well founded, that 1927 has seen the final overthrow of strict causality by Heisenberg, Bohr, Born and others, he year will certainly rank as one of the greatest epochs in the development of scientific philosophy.'

Mysticism usually frightens the people of a rational temper, chiefly because of the extravagances of some of its devotees. But the mysticism of Lao tzu, Whitman, and Eddington need not. Mathematics, the tool of science, works with equations and has yielded us nothing but equations, plus the new knowledge of the essential emptiness of matter. When Lao tzu and Chuang tzu spoke in mystic phraseology of the 'elusiveness' of Tao, it must be remembered that they were not being mystic, out merely good observers of life. For it must be remembered that it is exactly this quality of' elusiveness' of life processes that confronts the thinking scientist in his laboratory. The scientist knocks and the door refuses to open; at the moment he is about to discover the secret of life, life shuts up completely. He hunted matter and lost it in the electron: he hunted life and lost it in protoplasm; he hunted consciousness and lost it in electric brainwaves. Over and against his mathematical equations stood out clear, resistant, unbreakable, the sphere of meaning, beauty, love and consciousness, for which there are no tools for scientific exploration. Intuitive knowledge and mathematical knowledge never meet, for they obviously lie on different planes. Mathematics is a tool of the human mind and a way of expressing what the mind can see and reason about physical phenomena, and nothing more. Intuitive knowledge is different from, and is not subordinate to, mathematical or symbolic knowledge, as expressed in equations. Professor F. S. C. Northrop of Yale calls attention to the importance of recognising the place of intuitive knowledge of 'the aesthetic undifferentiated continuum,' and the right to existence of that kind of knowledge which is in all probability closer to reality than the differentiated knowledge of the reasoning mind, and which is exactly what Lao tzu meant when he warned against the danger of 'cutting up.' Chuang tzu is especially specific:

'The disadvantage of regarding things in separate parts is that when one begins to cut up and analyse, each one tries to be exhaustive The disadvantage of trying to be exhaustive is that it is consciously(mechanically) exhaustive. One goes on deeper and deeper, forgetting to return and sees a ghost (the externals of things only). Or one goes on and imagines he has got it, and what he has got is only a carcass For a thing which retains its substance but has lost the magic touch of life is but a ghost (of reality). Only one who can imagine the formless in the formed can arrive at the truth,'

By necessity, the physicist must carefully confine himself to observable forms, substances and motions, phenomena amenable to mathematical calculations, and in loyalty to his subject he consciously shuts his eyes to phenomena that are not mathematically manageable--the phenomena of life, mind, consciousness which must remain the eternal residue of science.

Fortunately for us, lying even more entirely outside the sphere of science, i.e., strictly 'illegitimate territory,' is the sphere of meanings and values. In this sense, Eddington draws the important distinction between the 'symbolic knowledge' (of science) and the 'intimate knowledge' of everyday experience. Eddington cleverly refutes critics who would call his mystical view 'nonsense,' or perhaps even 'damned nonsense.' 'What is the physical basis of nonsense?' he asks. Other critics may have the right to speak of 'nonsense,' but the positivist has no right to do so, because the word nonsense implies value, which is not legitimate within the logic of science, and damned nonsense implies even more value. 'In a world of ether and electrons we might perhaps encounter nonsense; we could not possibly encounter *damned nonsense.*' And so, fortunately, the world of meaning and value still remains with us. 'As scientists we realise that colour is merely a question of the wave-lengths of ethereal vibrations; but that does not seem to have dispelled the feeling that eyes which reflect light near wave-length 4,800 are a subject for rhapsody while those which reflect wave-length 5,300 are left unsung.'

Robert A. Millikan, dean of American scientists, made a striking and, to my mind, very important statement on religion when he read a paper before the American Physical Society, on April 29, 1947.

'A purely materialistic philosophy is to me the height of unintelligence. Wise men in all ages have always seen enough to at least make them reverent. Let me quote Einstein's notable words: "It is enough for me to contemplate the mystery of conscious life perpetuating itself through all eternity; to reflect upon the marvellous structure of the universe, which we can dimly perceive, and to try humbly to comprehend even an infinitesimal part of the intelligence manifested in nature."

That is as good a definition of God as I need

'I take credit for a few wise decisions myself, and why not? For while the Great Architect had to direct alone the earlier stages of the evolutionary process, that part of Him that became us for we are certainly inside, not outside, creation's plan-has been stepping up amazingly the pace of vegetable, animal and human evolution since we began to become conscious of the part we had to play. It is our sense of responsibility for playing our part to the best of our ability that makes us godlike.'

It seems that the great truths of the world have been seen by the wise men of all ages, regardless of country and period. Dr Millikan, Einstein, Eddington, Emerson, Lao tzu and Chuang tzu, with different backgrounds and possessing different tools of knowledge, come back to nearly the same thing. The preceding statement of belief is, I believe, acceptable to most thinking modern men. But the ideas are characteristically Taoist: "It is enough for me to contemplate, etc.,' 'the intelligence manifested in nature,' 'which we can *dimly perceive*,' and that part of Him that became us.' Emerson, too, says he was a part of 'God in nature.'

What Emerson wrote a hundred years ago is still true today. 'We have the same need to command a view of the religion of the world. We can never see Christianity from the catechism-from the pastures, from a boat in the pond, from a midst the songs of wood-birds we possibly may. That is about where we stand today, possibly all we need. And Lao tzu adds, 'He who does not think so-his door of divine intelligence is shut.'

IV

In 1942, I translated the *Book of Tao* and eleven out of the thirty-three chapters of Chuang tzu, included in *The Wisdom of China*. In the present work, I have revised these translations in places, and have made new translations of the other parts of Chuang tzu. Although the selections consist of extracts only, they may be considered fairly representative of Chuang tzu's writing and ideas. The revision of the Book of Tao entails only minor changes, chiefly substituting the terms "'humanity' and 'character' where love' and 'virtue' were used. I have here attempted a new division of the Book of Tao into seven books which I believe will be of some help to the reader in grasping the essential idea of each group of chapters. Roughly speaking, the first forty chapters deal with the principles of the philosophy, the rest with its applications in human problems. In the comments on the selections from Chuang tzu, I have confined myself to an editor's job of making the connections clear, and pointing up an emphasis here and there, but have otherwise not attempted to express my opinions. For a proper introduction to the intellectual background of the period of Lao tzu and Chuang tzu, and particularly for a characterization of the ideas of the two philosophers by Chuang tzu himself, see the Prolegomena.

Prolegomena

'The Main Currents of Thought'

by Chuang tzu

It is useful to know something of the intellectual background of China at the time of Lao tzu and Chuang tzu and the diversity of schools of thinking out of which their philosophy arose. But so little of the Chinese literature of ideas has been made available to the West that believe a translation of this valuable document by Chuang tzu will be more appreciated than a survey written by a modern writer.

The essay called 'The World' (from the first two words at the beginning) was written in the brilliant style of Chuang tzu, succinct, critical and packed with thought, and gives a very valuable outline of the main schools of thinking current in his time. It is interesting to note that in this summary of current thought, the Confucians and Yang Chu's school are conspicuous by their absence, and that while Liehtse figures in the works of Chuang tzu as a person gifted with magical powers, he is not mentioned in this essay as a Taoist philosopher. I have arranged the division into sections and section headings for the convenience of the reader.

It will be especially seen from Section 3 that many of the Taoist ideas expressed by Lao tzu and Chuang tzu, such as the concept of an impersonal Tao, repudiation of knowledge and acceptance of the laws of the nature, were current in Chuang tzu's day in the group known as the 'Temple of God of Grain philosophers,' a name taken from the place in Ch'i where the group associated with one another.

Chuang tzu's listing of his own name and his self-appraisal are not proper reasons for doubting that the essay was written by himself, if one knows his character well.

Roughly speaking, the groups 1, 2 and 6 represent the Motsearns, with the Neo-Motsearns described in 1 and 6, while groups 3, 4 and 5 represent the Taoist trend of thinking.

Many are the professors of philosophies of order and government in the world today. Each school regards itself as having found the best. It may be asked: In what school is to be found the philosophy of the ancients? The answer is that it is to be found in every system. Questions are asked: Whence comes the spirit and how did consciousness arise? The Sage's wisdom, must have a source, and the king's power must derive from some-thing. The source of both is the One (of the universe).

(I) *The scope of ancient philosophy*. He who does not deviate from the source of all things is a man of God. He who does not deviate from the Essence is a divine person. He who does not deviate from the Truth is a perfect man. He who regard the Heaven as the source, **Teh** as the foundation, and **Tao** as he portal, which is evidenced in all the changes of life, is a Sage. He who guides himself by the principle of humanity in performing acts of kindness, follows justice as his principle observes ceremony for his conduct, expresses the sense of harmony by means of music, and thus becomes compassionate and kind--he is a gentleman.

Regulation by law, distinction by ranks and titles, verification by comparing evidences and reaching a decision after due investigation, being always specific with 'one,' 'two,' 'three', 'four'- these are means (of administration) by which officials carry out their duties in order. To start out with the business of daily living, whose principal occupations are food and clothing to grow and multiply and save, so that the old and the young and the widow and the orphan shall be well provided for-these are the fundamental needs of the people.

The ancients provided adequately for all this. From serving God and sacrificing to heaven and earth, to the art of letting all things grow, making the people live in peace, and benefiting he people, the ancients understood both the principles and their applications. All points of space and all conditions of time, from the small to the big, and from the subtle to the gross, are within the compass (of their philosophy). Many of the history books recording the old laws and traditions still exist. As regards poetry, history, ceremony and music, many of the scholars of Tsou and Lu (districts of Mencius and Confucius) and the intelligentsia understand them. Poetry serves to communicate the hearts and hopes of men; history records events; the science of ceremonies discusses conduct; music expresses harmony of spirit; the "Book of Changes' tells about yin and pang; and the Spring and Autumn Annals' discusses social status and duties. All this body of knowledge, scattered about the world and found in China, is often pointed out and discussed by the various schools of philosophers.

(Now) the world is in universal chaos. The ways of the wise and the sage are not understood, and **Tao** and **Teh** are taught in different ways. Many philosophers emphasise one particular aspect and hold on to it. It is like a person whose senses function properly each in its own field, but do not co-operate with one another, or again like the artisans of different trades who are" good each in his own line and are often needed. However, without an adequate comprehension of the whole, these are but one-alley scholars. In their appreciation of the beauty of the universe, their analysis of the principles of the creation, and in their study of the entirety of the ancient men's thoughts, they seldom comprehend adequately the beauty of the universe and the ways of the spirit. Hence the principles of the authorities of thought and of government are hidden in the dark and find no proper expression. Each man thinks what he likes and creates his own system. Alas, gone astray are the various schools of philosophy, without being able to find their way back. They shall never find the truth. The scholars of posterity, unfortunately, shall not be able to see the original simplicity of the universe and the main foundation of thought of the ancients. Philosophy is thus cut up and falls apart.

(1) *The Ascetics, the followers of Mo Ti[1] (or Motse)*. Some of the teachings of the ancients lay in this: not to strive for posthumous fame, not to waste the things of the earth, not to be dazzled by laws and institutions, but to be severe with one-self and hold oneself ready to help others in need. Mo Ti and Ch'in Huali heard of these teachings and loved them. (They)tended to overdo it, regarding it as a great satisfaction. (Motse)wrote the essay 'Against Music,' and taught: 'Be thrifty. Do not sing in life, and do not mourn in death.' Motse taught universal love and the principle of benefiting all people, and he preached against war. Anger is unknown in his teachings. Besides, he loved learning and was widely read like the others. He would not accept (the tradition of) the ancient kings, and wanted to destroy the ceremonies and music of the ancients, such as the Hsiench'ih (name of sacrificial music) of the Yellow Emperor, the Tachang of Yao, the Tashao of Shun, the Tahsia of Yu, the Tahu of T'ang, the P'iyung of King Wen and the Wu of King Wu and Duke Chou. In the ancient funeral ceremonies, there was definite distinction of rank and position The body of an emperor was laid in a seven-fold coffin, those of the princes and dukes, five-fold, those of the noblemen three-fold, and those of the scholars without rank, double. Motse taught that one should not sing in life and should not mourn in death and prescribed a single coffin three inches thick as the rule for all alike. Such teachings are hard on the teacher himself and on others who practice it. But it has not made them the less popular.

1 Motse undoubtedly lived between 501 and 416 B.C. See my introduction to,Motse. Wisdom of China. pp. 217-219.

However, what kind of a teaching is this, when one must not sing when he wants to sing, must not weep when he wants to weep, and must not enjoy music when he is feeling happy? It causes a man to live strenuously and die cheaply, and must be considered too severe. It also makes men sad and austere and is a doctrine difficult to practice. I am afraid this is not the teaching of the sages. For it goes against human nature, and few people can stand it. Though Motse was able to live it him-self, what about the great majority of men? When a teaching sets itself apart from common humanity, it must be regarded as far from the way to set the world in order.

Motse used to say, "When Emperor Yu was fighting the deluge, channelling the water into rivers and guiding its course through the four barbarian territories and nine continents there were three hundred mountains and three thousand tributaries in the entire domain, besides innumerable smaller ones. With his own hands he plied the shovel and dredger, to channel all the streams toward the great rivers, until the hair on his calves and shins were worn off. His body was bathed in heavy rain and his hair was combed by strong winds, and yet he marked out the (boundaries of) the districts. Yu was a great sage, and yet he laboured so hard for the world.' Because of such teachings, the Motseans in later generations wear hide jackets and wooden or straw sandals, working day and nigh without cease to torture themselves, saying, 'Unless I do so, Is hall not be following the teachings of Yu and shall be unworthy of a Motsean.'

The disciples of Hsiangli Ch'in and the followers of the five counts are the Motseans of the south. People like K'u Huo, Chi Ch'ih and Teng Lingtse all studied the canon of Motse but they differ among themselves and call themselves 'Neo Motseans.' They (the sophists) dispute among themselves about the nature of) hardness, whiteness, similarity and difference and talk in strange and contradictory terms. They regard Chutse as their sage and all desire to be his spiritual successor so as to obtain control of his following. Even now the questions not settled. Mo Ti and Ch'in Huali meant well by their teachings, but the results are deplorable. It is inevitable that his later followers should all try to torture themselves and wear the hair off their calves and shins in competition for merit. 'The good they did outweighs the harm they have done. However, it cannot be denied that Motse was really an excellent character, of which we have too few examples in this world. Despite all personal hardships, he lived what he preached. Indeed, he was distinguished among men.

(2) Teachers of Mercy: Sung Hsing[2] and Yin Wen. Some of the teachings of the ancients lay in this: Not to be burdened with material possessions, not to show off before people, not to be indifferent to others, and not to be critical of the masses, desiring that all men may live in peace and their lives be saved, the sole aim being to see that all people are well provided for. Sung Hsing and Yin Wen heard of such teachings and loved them. They wear the 'Huashan (flat-top) cap' to distinguish themselves. In all their dealings with people, they start with consideration for others and forgiveness. They speak of the tolerance of the human heart and call it `conduct coming from the heart.' Wearing a kindly, peaceful appearance, they go about preaching to the world, saying that this should be made the dominant teaching for all. When insulted, they do not take offence, and they try to prevent people from fighting. They are against offensive wars and for disarmament, hoping to stop the wars in the world. With such teachings, they go about the world, and talk to the officials and the commoners, and though people will not listen to them, they never stop harping upon them. Therefore it is said that everybody is bored with them and they still insist on interviewing people. However, they live too much for others and too little for themselves. (Addressing themselves as 'disciples' and the other person as 'master') they would say, 'Master, give us only five pints of rice; it will be enough. We are afraid you have not enough for yourself. We don't mind going hungry, for we have the world to think about.' Thus they go on day and night and say, 'Somehow I am sure we can survive.' They appear rather to put to shame the saviours of the world. They teach that a gentleman should not be critical of others, or make oneself slave of one's possessions and attend to affairs which are of no benefit to the world and thus they show others' way of life to disadvantage. They regard banning offensive wars and retiring all soldiers as the issues of the day, but to have simple desires is the principle of self-cultivation. Such in general are the principles and details of their belief and conduct.

2 Lived between 370 and 291, and thus was a contemporary of Chuangtse. Alsoknown as Sung Yung.

(3) *The Taoists of Chi (the 'Temple of God of Grain group'),P'eng Meng, T'ien P'ien, and Shen Tao.* Some of the teachings of the ancients lay in this: Be impartial and do not belong to any party, be natural and selfless, make yourself completely free and not bound to any objective, take things as they come, with-out worry or concern and without putting faith in cleverness,accept all and mingle with all. P'eng Meng, T'ien P'ien and Shen Tao heard of these teachings and loved them. Their fundamental idea is the levelling of all things. These people teach: Heaven shelters, but cannot support things; the earth supports, but cannot shelter things. The great Tao encompasses all, but this Tao cannot be explained. They realise that the different things all have their capacities and limitations. There-fore, they say, to mention a particular is always to miss the whole, and teaching cannot ever explain the ultimate truth, but Tao includes everything. Therefore Shen Tao rejects know-ledge and the self, and does only what is inevitable, being detached towards all things as his guiding principle. One who knows does not really know, says he, and a little knowledge is the beginning of injury (to the wholeness of one's character).Being wayward and irresponsible, he laughs at the value placed upon the wise men of the world, and being carefree and unrestrained, he abuses the great sages. In a rule-of-the-thumb, haphazard way he deals with things as they come, Taking no sides of a question, he manages to survive. Taking no thought of what comes before or after, and placing no faith in planning and contriving, he remains impressively himself. He has to be pushed before he will move and dragged before he will take a step, and he seems to float along, going round and round like whirlwind, or a feather in the wind, or again like a turning grind stone. Yet he manages to escape criticism, and never seems to take a wrong step or violate the law. What is the reason? For animals without reason never stop to think for themselves or burden their minds with deliberations; they act always in accordance with nature, and thus are for ever free from criticism. Therefore he teaches: be like the animals without reason; have no use for the sages and wise men; even a clod of earth behaves in accordance with Tao. The knowing critics would say, 'The teachings of Shen Tao are fit

for the dead, not for the living. The only result is to make one peculiar.'

Tien P'ien is also like that. He studied under P'eng Meng and leaned what could not be taught. P'eng Meng's teacher used to say, 'All the ancient followers of Tao tried to do was to reach the state beyond praise or blame. Such subtle truths are beyond expression by words.' They often express opinions the opposite of others, which are seldom appreciated, yet they cannot help making stop-gap judgments. What they regard as Tao is not Tao, and what they consider as right is often wrong. P'eng Meng, T'ien P'ien and Shen Tao do not really understand Tao (as philosophical principle), but understand some of it.

(4) Lao tzu (Lao Tan) and Kuan Yin.[3] Some of the teachings of the ancients lay in this: the root of all things is subtle, while the material things are gross (appearances of reality); all measurable quantities fall short of the truth of reality; live calmly and dispassionately alone with the spirits. Lao tzu and Kuan Yin heard of such teachings and loved them. Their

---

3 Kuan Yin must not be confused with 'Kwanyin,' the Buddhist Goddess of Mercy. It was the name of an officer, 'Commander of the Pass,' the person who, according to tradition, persuaded Lao tzu to write his book.

fundamental thesis is that not-being is the constant phase (of life), and all things can be traced to the Great One. They teach gentleness and humility in appearance, and a passive attitude and the belief that one should not destroy the things of the universe (by interference) as the substance (of their faith). Kuan Yin says, 'If you get away from your (subjective) point of view, things and forms will appear in their true light by themselves. One's movements should be like water, his state of rest like the (passive) mirror, and his response to surroundings like an echo to the sound. Be illusive, appearing as if not to exist; be still, appearing like clear water. Who accepts things merges with them; who makes things, breaks. Do not ever put yourself forward, but always follow behind.' Lao Tan (Lao tzu) says, 'Be aware of the male, but keep to the female and be the (hollow) valley of the earth. Be aware of the white, but keep to the tarnished, and be the ravine of the world.' 'Others reach for the first place; I take the last.' Again he says, "Receive unto yourself the calumny of the world.' 'Others strive for the substance, I rather choose the passive void.' 'Because one does not hoard, one has abundance, indeed great is his abundance.' His way of life is slow and easy and not wasteful of energy; he believed in doing nothing and laughed at those who do things. Others pray for good luck, he alone was content with being wronged, saying, 'Thus may I hope to be free from reproach. He believes in depth for one's foundation, and simplicity as the main teaching of conduct. He says, The hard will break, and the sharp-edged will be blunted. Be tolerant of all and you will not be hurt.' Such teachings may be considered indeed the height of all knowledge. Kuan Yin and Lao tzu were the great pure men of ancient days.

(5) *Chuang Chou (Chuang tzu)*. Some of the teachings of the ancients lay in this: reality is ever elusive and formless, and all life is constant change. What are life and death? Am I one with the universe? Where do the spirits move? Whither do they go, and where do they disappear, so mysteriously and suddenly? The creation lies spread before me, but in none of these things can be found the true source. Chuang Chou heard of such teachings and loved them. With unbridled fancies, facetious language and sweet romantic nonsense, he gives free play to his spirit without restraint. He cannot be understood from any detached sayings of his. He regards the world as hopelessly sunk in a muddle, unworthy to talk with Chou (himself). His goblet words are a continual pouring forth, his 'serious words' are true, and his 'allegories' are broad in implications. Alone he stands with the heaven and earth and wanders as a companion of the spirits. But he does not despise the things of the universe, or quarrel about what others regard as right and wrong, and he mingles with conventional society. Although his books dazzle and spin out lengthy discourses, this is a minor blemish. Though his language is uneven (shifting from the serious to the facetious), it is lively and good reading, for it overflows from the fullness of his thoughts and he cannot stop himself. Above, his spirit wanders with the Creator, and below he makes friends with those who transcend life and death and beginning and end. The foundation of his thought is big and wide, deep and unconfined. The core of his teachings can encompass all phenomena and reach up to the divine order. However, in its adjustment to the changing life and under-standing of physical things, its principle is inexhaustible, traceless, dark and formless, and it is difficult to get hold of.

(6) *Huei Shil and the sophists*. Huei Shih was versatile in his knowledge, and his books filled five carts. His teachings are peculiar and his sayings miss the truth. In speaking of the nature of the physical universe, he says, 'The extreme of bigness has no limit; this is called the infinite. The extreme of smallness has no core; this is called the infinitesimal. There is no limit to accumulated distance, which extends to thousands of miles. Heaven is as low as the earth, and mountains and lakes are on the same level. When the sun is at the zenith, it is setting(somewhere else); when a thing is alive, it (begins to) die. The differences between sub-classes in a class are called the lesser differences and similarities. All things differ and yet all are alike; these are called the greater differences and similarities. There is no limit and vet there is a limit in the direction of the south (*relativity of space*). One starts out for Yueh today and arrives there yesterday (*relativity of time*). Joined rings can be detached (*for they are detached*). I know the centre of the universe. North of Yen (in north China) is south of Yueh (*in south China; assuming roundness of the earth*).' Such are examples of his teachings. He loves all creation and considers the universe as one. Huei Shih tries to enlighten the logicians with his view of the universe, and the logicians of the day love it. (Such are some of his sophistries): The egg contains hair (latent in the embryo). A chicken has three legs (two plus the will which moves them). Ying (a small country) possesses the world (being identical in nature with the rest). A dog can be a sheep and a horse lays eggs all being questions of nomenclature). The frog has a tail (though it is atrophied). Fire is not hot (heat being subjective). Mountains have mouths (they echo). The wheel never touches the ground (except one point at a time). The eye does not see (for it is the brain which does). The finger does not point to a thing, but rather points endlessly beyond it. The tortoise is longer than the snake(relativity of notions of size). The carpenter's square does no 'make' a square, and his compass dos not 'make' a circle (*he latter being independent squares and circles*). The mortice does not surround the bit of a chisel (there being always space between the two). The shadow of a flying bird never moves (*being in reality a succession of individual shadows*). There is a

point of time when the head of a flying arrow neither moves nor stops. A watch-dog is not a dog (*the terms being not co-extensive*). A bay horse and a dun cow make three (*two plus colour*). A white dog is black (depending on what one means by whiteness and blackness)A motherless colt never had a mother (which is but a notion at the time when it has no mother). Take a stick one foot long and cut it in half every day and you will never come to the end even after ten thousand years.

    The logicians devote all their lives discussing these points with Huei Shih. These logicians, like Huan T'uan and Kungsun Lung, please men's minds and influence men's thinking. They are able to worst others by argument, but do not convince people in their hearts, because they are just play in ground with words. And thus Huei Shih daily exercises his wit to argue with people and makes a show of it with other sophists of the day. The above is a brief summary.

However, Huei Shih is very proud of his eloquence. He says, 'Great is the universe!' Shih likes to excel others, but he lacks a fundamental belief. Once there was a man from the south by the name of Huang Liao, who asked him why the sky did not fall down and the earth did not drop off, and who questioned him on the reasons for the wind and the rain and thunder, and Huei Shih was able to answer him without a moment's thinking. He talks about everything in the universe without end and without limit, and yet he thinks he has not talked enough, but goes on saying stranger and stranger things. Because he contradicts what others regard as true and overcomes them with words, his opinions are not accepted by many. Weak in his understanding of **Teh** (character or spiritual constitution) and engrossed with material things, he gets lost in the bypaths. From the point of view of the universe, Huei Shib's intellectual exercises are but as the activities of a humming mosquito or a buzzing gadfly. Of what use are his teachings to the world? It should be enough to recognize the One and talk a little less, thus approaching the Tao. Huei Shih cannot content himself with this, but scatters his mind over the physical things without ever getting tired, and ends up with a reputation as a good logician. Alas, Huei Shih wastes his talent and ends up holding nothing. He buries himself in physical things and cannot find his way back, like one trying to drown an echo with his voice, or like a man running away from his own shadow. This is sad indeed!

BOOK ONE

THE CHARACTER OF TAO

1. ON THE ABSOLUTE TAO

The Tao that can be told of
Is not the Absolute Tao;
The Names that can be given
Are not Absolute Names.

The Nameless is the origin of Heaven and Earth;
The Named is the Mother of All Things.

Therefore:
Oftentimes, one strips oneself of passion
    In order to see the Secret of Life;
Oftentimes, one regards life with passion
    In order to see its manifest forms.

These two (the Secret and its manifestations)
Are (in their nature) the same;
They are given different names
When they become manifest.

They may both be called the Cosmic Mystery:[1]
Reaching from the Mystery into the Deeper Mystery
Is the Gate to the secret[2] of All Life

1 Hsuan-This word is the equivalent of 'mystic' and 'mysticism.' Taoism is also known as the Hsian chiao, or "Mystic Religion.
2 Miao may also be translated as 'Essence'; it means 'the wonderful,' the 'ultimate,' the 'logically unknowable,' the 'quintessence,' or 'esoteric truth'.

The numbered sections, 1.1, 1.2, 1.3, 1.4, etc., are translations of elections from Chuang tzu which bear on the chapter. The number in parentheses at the end of each selection indicate the volume and page number of the Sweeping Leaves Lodge Chinese edition of Chuang tzu: '6.4' means volume 6 page 4. Chapter numbers are not indicated because the chapters are usually very long and they are not suitable for quick reference. Students who wish to obtain the chapter numbers from the volume and page references may consult the Conversion Table at the back.

1.1. THE TAO THAT CANNOT BE NAMED, TOLD OR DISCUSSED
Therefore Ether asked Infinite, "Do you know Tao?"
'I don't know,' replied Infinite.
He asked No-action the same question and No-action replied. I know Tao.
'So you know Tao. Can you specify?'
'Certainly.'
'I know that Tao can be high, can be low, can be centred and can be dispersed. These are some of the specifications that I know.'
Ether told No-beginning of No-action's words and asked,
' Thus Infinite says he does not know and No-action says he knows. Who is right?'
'The one who thinks he does not know is profound, and the one who thinks he knows is shallow. The former deals with the inner reality, the latter with appearance.'
Ether raised his head and sighed: 'Then one who does not know really knows, and one who knows really does not know Who knows this knowledge without knowing?'
'Tao cannot be heard,' said No-beginning, 'that which is heard is not Tao. Tao cannot be seen; that which is seen is not Tao. Tao cannot be told; that which can be told is not Tao. Do you realize that which is invisible in all the visible things? Tao should not be named.'

And No-beginning said, 'If someone answers in reply to question about Tao. he does not know Tao. Even the one who asks about Tao has not heard Tao. Tao cannot be asked about,and to the question there is no answer. To ask about that which should not be asked is to land in extremities. To answer a question which should not be answered is to fail to recognize the inner reality. If then those who do not recognize the inner reality try to answer questioners who land in extremities, such people have neither observed the workings of the universe, nor do they realize the Ultimate Source. Therefore they cannot surmount the Kunlun Mountains and travel in the realm of the Great Void.' (6:4)

On the impossibility of naming or describing Tao see also Ch. 25.

1.2. THE CONDITIONED AND THE UNCONDITIONED.
The knowledge of the men of old reached the ultimate height. What was the ultimate height of knowledge? They recognized that nothing but nothing existed. That indeed was the limit further than which one could not go. Then there were those who believed that matter existed, but only matter unconditioned (undefined).Next came those who believed in conditioned (defined) matter but did not recognize the distinctions of true and false. When the distinctions of true and false appeared, then Tao lost its wholeness. And when Tao lost its wholeness, individual bias began. (1:7)

1.3. ALL THINGS ARE ONE. THE EYE OF THE SENSES AND THE EYE OF THE SPIRIT.
In the State of Lu there was a man, named Wang T'ai, who had had one of his legs cut off. His disciples were as numerous as those of Confucius.

Ch'ang Chi asked Confucius, saying, 'This Wang T'ai has been mutilated, yet he has as many followers in the Lu State as you. He neither stands up to preach nor sits down to give discourse; yet those who go to him empty, depart full. Is he the kind of person who can teach without words and influence people's minds without material means? What manner of man is this?'

'He is a sage,' replied Confucius. 'I wanted to go to him, but am merely behind the others. Even I will go and make him my teacher-why not those who are lesser than I? And I will lead, not only the State of Lu, but the whole world to follow him.' 'The man has been mutilated,' said Ch'ang Chi, 'and yet people call him "Master." He must be very different from the ordinary men. If so, how does he train his mind?'

'Life and Death are indeed changes of great moment,' answered Confucius, 'but they cannot affect his mind. ... It can control the transformation of things, while preserving its source intact.'
'How so?' asked Ch'ang Chi.
'From the point of view of differentiation of things,' replied Confucius, 'we distinguish between the liver and the gall, between the Ch'u State and the Yueh State. From the point of view of their sameness, all things are One. He who regards things in this light does not trouble about what reaches him through the senses of hearing and sight, but lets his mind wander in the moral harmony of things. He beholds the unity in things, and does not notice the loss of particular objects. And thus the loss of his leg is to him as would be the loss of so much dirt'(2:1)

Therefore what he (the pure man) cared for was One, and what he did not care for was also (parts, manifestations of) One. What he saw as One was One, and what he saw as not One was also One. In that he saw the unity, he was of God; in that he saw the distinctions, he was of man. Not to allow the human and the divine to be confused, therein was what distinguished the pure man.

Life and Death are a part of Destiny. Their sequence, like day and night, is of God, beyond the interference of man. These all lie in the inevitable nature of things. He simply looks upon God as his father; if he loves him with what is born of the body, shall he not love him also with that which is greater than the body? A man looks upon a ruler of men as one superior to himself; if he is willing to sacrifice his body (for his ruler)shall he not then offer his pure (spirit) also?

When the pond dries up and fish are left upon the dry ground, rather than leave them to moisten one another with their spittle, it would be better to let them lose themselves in their native rivers and lakes. Rather than praise Yao and blame Chieh, it would be better to forget both (the good and the bad) and lose oneself in Tao.

The Great (universe) gives me this form, this toil in man-hood, this repose in old age, this rest in death. Surely that which is such a kind arbiter of my life is the best arbiter of my death. (2:5)

1.4. THE GATE TO THE SECRET OF ALL LIFE.

When (Tao)appears, one cannot see its root; when (Tao) disappears, one cannot see its concrete forms. It has substance, but is not con-fined in space; it has length, but its source cannot be traced Since it can manifest itself and yet disappear without concrete forms, it must have substance. Having substance and yet being not confined-that is space. Having length and yet being without source-that is time. And so there is life and death, and appearance and disappearance. To appear and disappear without showing its form-that is the Gate of Heaven. The Gate of Heaven signifies non-being.

All things come from non being.(6:8)

2. THE RISE OF RELATIVE OPPOSITES

When the people of the Earth all know beauty as beauty,
There arises (the recognition of) ugliness.
When the people of the Earth all know the good as good,
There arises (the recognition of) evil.
Therefore:
Being and non-being interdepend in growth;
Difficult and easy interdepend in completion;
Long and short interdepend in contrast;
High and low interdepend in position;
Tones and voice interdepend in harmony;
Front and behind interdepend in company.
Therefore the Sage:

Manages affairs without action;
Preaches the doctrine without words;
All things take their rise, but he does not turn away from them;
He gives them life, but does not take possession of them;
He acts, but does not appropriate Accomplishes. but claims no credit.
It is because he lays claim to no credit,
That the credit cannot be taken away from him.

The principle of the levelling of all opposites, and the theory of cycles and universal reversion to opposites, see Ch. 40, are basic for the understanding of Lao tzu and Chuang tzu philosophy and its practical teachings. All Lao tzu's paradoxes arise from this point of view.

2.1. THE RELATIVITY OF OPPOSITES. THE LEVELING OF ALL THINGS AND ATTRIBUTES INTO ONE. For speech is not mere blowing of breath. It is intended to say something, only what it is intended to say cannot yet be determined. Is there speech indeed, or is there not? Can we, or can we not, distinguish it from the chirping of young birds?

How can Tao be so obscured that there should be a distinction of true and false? How can speech be so obscured that there should be a distinction of right and wrong?[3] Where can you go and find Tao not to exist? Where can you go and find that words cannot be proved? Tao is obscured by our inadequate understanding, and words are obscured by flowery expressions. Hence the affirmations and denials of the Confucian and Motsean[4] schools, each denying what the other affirms and affirming what the other denies. Each denying what the other affirms and affirming what the other denies brings us only confusion.

3 Shih and fei mean general moral judgments and mental distinctions: 'right' and 'wrong,' 'true' and 'false,' 'is' and 'is not,' 'affirmative' and 'negative,' also to' justify' and 'condemn,' to 'affirm' and 'deny.'
4 The followers of Motse were powerful rivals of the Confucians in Chuang tzu's day.

There is nothing which is not this; there is nothing which is not that. What cannot be seen by that (the other person) can be known by myself. Hence I say, this emanates from that; that also derives from this. This is the theory of the interdependence of *this* and *that* (relativity of standards).

Nevertheless, life arises from death, and *vice versa*.

Possibility arises from impossibility, and *vice versa*.

Affirmation is based upon denial, and *vice versa*.

Which being the case, the true Sage rejects all distinctions and takes his refuge in Heaven. or one may base it on this, yet this is also that and that is also this. This also has its 'right' and 'wrong,' and that also has it 'right' and 'wrong.' Does then the distinction between this and that really exist or not? When this (subjective) and that (objective) are both without their correlates, that is the very 'Axis of Tao.' And when that Axis passes through the centre at which all infinities converge, affirmations and denials alike blend into the infinite One. Hence it is said that there is nothing like using the Light.

To take a finger in illustration of a finger not being a finger is not so good as to take something which is not a finger to illustrate that a finger is not a finger. To take a horse in illustration of a horse not being a horse is not so good as to take something which is not a horse to illustrate that a horse is not horse.[5] So with the universe which is but a finger, but a horse The possible is possible: the impossible is impossible. Tao operates, and given results follow; things receive names and are said to be what they are. Why are they so? They are said to be so! Why are they not so? They are said to be not so Things are so by themselves and have possibilities by them-selves. There is nothing which is not so and there is nothing which may not become so.

5 The meaning of these two sentences is made clear below. 'But if we put the different categories in one, then the differences of category cease to exist.' See selection 2.3.

Therefore take, for instance, a twig and a pillar, or an ugly person and a great beauty, and all the strange and monstrous, transformations. These are all levelled together by Tao. Division is the same as creation; creation is the same as destruction There is no such thing as creation or destruction, for these conditions are again levelled together into One.

Only the truly intelligent understand this principle of the levelling of all things into One. They discard the distinctions and take refuge in the common and ordinary things. The common and ordinary things serve certain functions and therefore retain the wholeness of nature. From this wholeness, on comprehends, and from comprehension, one comes near to Tao. There one stops. To stop without knowing how one stops-this is Tao.(1:5,6)

2.2. THE RELATIVITY OF ALL STANDARDS. DEPENDENCE ON SUBJECTIVE VIEWPOINT

'But how then,' asked the Spirit of the River, 'arise the distinctions of high and low, of great and small, in the material and immaterial aspects of things?'

From the point of view of Tao,' replied the Spirit of the Ocean, 'there are no such distinctions of high and low. From the point of view of individuals, each holds himself high and others low. From the vulgar point of view, high and low honour and dishonour) are things conferred by others.

'In regard to distinctions, if we say that a thing is great or small by its own standard of great or small,then there is nothing in all creation which is not great, nothing which is not small To know that the universe is but as a tare-seed, and the tip of a hair is (as big as) a mountain-this is the expression of relativity of standards.

'In regard to function, if we say that something exists or does not exist, by its own standard of existence or non-existence,hen there is nothing which does not exist, nothing which does not perish from existence. If we know that east and west are convertible and yet necessary terms, in relation to each other then such (relative) functions may be established.

'In regard to man's desires or interests, if we say that a thing is good or bad because it is either good or bad according to our individual (subjective) standards, then there is nothing which is not good, nothing which is not bad. If we know that Yao and Chieh each regarded himself as good and the other as bad.hen the (direction of) their interests becomes apparent....

'Thus, those who say that they would have right without its correlate, wrong, or good government without its correlate. misrule, do not apprehend the great principles of the universe, nor the nature of all creation. One might as well talk of the existence of Heaven without that of Earth, or of the negative principle without the positive, which is clearly impossible. Yet people keep on discussing it without stop; such people must be either fools or knaves.'

'Very well,' replied the Spirit of the River, 'am I then to regard the universe as great and the tip of a hair as small?'

'Not at all,' said the Spirit of the Ocean. 'Dimensions are limitless; time is endless. Conditions are not constant; external limits are not final. Thus, the wise man looks into space, and does not regard the small as too little, nor the great as too big;for he knows that there is no limit to dimensions. He looks back into the past, and does not grieve over what is far off, no rejoice over what is near; for he knows that time is without end. He investigates fullness and decay, and therefore does not rejoice if he succeeds, nor lament if he fails; for he knows that conditions are not constant. He who clearly apprehends the scheme of existence does not rejoice over life, nor repine at death; for he knows that external limits are not final.'

2.3. THE FUTILITY OF LANGUAGE. ON PREACHING THE DOCTRINE WITHOUT WORDS.

Suppose here is a statement. We do not know whether it belongs to one category or another. But if we put the different categories in one, then the differences of category cease to exist. However, I must explain. If there was, a beginning, then there was a time before that beginning, and a time before the time which was before the time of that beginning. If there is existence, there must have been non-existence. And if there was a time when nothing existed, then there must have been a time when even nothing did not exist. All of a sudden, nothing came into existence. Could one then really say whether it belongs to the category of existence or of non-existence? Even the very words I have just now uttered-I cannot say whether they say something or not.

There is nothing under the canopy of heaven greater than the tip of a bird's down in autumn, while the T'ai Mountain is small. Neither is there any longer life than that of a child cutoff in infancy, while P'eng Tsu himself died young. The universe and I came into being together; the myriad things of the creation and I are One.

If then all things are One, what room is there for speech? On the other hand, since I can say the word 'one' how can speech not exist? If it does exist, we have one and speech-two;and two and one-three from which point on even the best mathematicians will fail to reach (the ultimate); how much more then should ordinary people fail?

Hence, if from nothing you can proceed to something, and subsequently reach three, it follows that it would be still easier if you started from something. Since you cannot proceed, take your rest.

Now Tao by its very nature can never be defined. Speech by its very nature cannot express the absolute. Hence arise the distinctions. Such distinctions are: 'right' and 'left,' 'relationship' and 'duty,' 'division' and 'discrimination,' 'emulation' and 'contention.' These are called the Eight Predicables.

Beyond the limits of the external world, the Sage knows that it exists, but does not discuss it. Within the limits of the external world, the Sage discusses but does not pass judgments. With regard to the wisdom of the ancients, as embodied in the canon of *Spring and Autumn*, the Sage judges, but does not expound. And thus, among distinctions made, there are distinctions that cannot be made; among things expounded, there are things that cannot be expounded.

How can that be? it is asked. The true Sage keeps his knowledge within him, while the common men set forth theirs in argument, in order to convince each other. Therefore it is said that one who argues does so because he is confused.

Now perfect Tao cannot be given a name. A perfect argument does not employ words. Perfect kindness does not concern itself with (individual acts of) kindness. Perfect integrity is not critical of others. Perfect courage does not push itself forward.

For the Tao which is manifest is not Tao. Speech which argues falls short of its aim. Kindness which has fixed objects loses its scope. Integrity which is obvious is not believed in. Courage which pushes itself forward never accomplishes anything. These five are, as it were, round (mellow) with a strong bias towards squareness (sharpness). Therefore the knowledge which stops at what it does not know is the highest knowledge.

Who knows the argument which can be argued without words, and the Tao which does not declare itself as Tao? He who knows this may be said to have entered the realm of the spirit. [6]

6 Lit 'in the Palace of Heaven.'

Chuang tzu's idea of the futility of language is closely connected with his theory of knowledge of reality. 'He who knows does not talk, and he who talks does not know. Therefore the Sage preaches the doctrine without words.' (6:1) See Ch. 56.

The following passage was directed against the argumentative philosophers of Chuang tzu's time, especially the neo-Motseans, like Hwei Shih and Kungsun Lung.

2.4. THE FUTILITY OF ARGUMENT. Granting that you and I argue. If you get the better of me, and not I of you, are you necessarily right and I wrong? Or if I get the better of you and not you of me, am I necessarily right and you wrong? Or are we both partly right and partly wrong? Or are we both wholly right and wholly wrong? Since you and I cannot know, we all live in darkness.

Whom shall I ask to judge between us? If I ask someone who takes your view, he will side with you. How can such a one arbitrate between us? If I ask someone who takes my view, he will side with me. How can such a one arbitrate between us? If I ask someone who differs from both of us, he will be equally unable to decide between us, since he differs from both of us. And if I ask someone who agrees with both of us, he will be equally unable to decide between us, since he agrees with both of us. Since you and I and other men cannot decide, how can we depend upon another? The words of arguments are all relative; if we wish to reach the absolute, we must harmonise them by means of the unity of God, and follow their natural evolution to the end of our days.

But what is to harmonise them by means of the unity of God? It is this. The right may not be really right. What appear so may not be really so. Even if what is right is really right, wherein it differs from wrong cannot be made plain by argument. Even if what appears so is really so, wherein it differs from what is not so also cannot be made plain by argument. Take no heed of time nor of right and wrong. Passing into the realm of the Infinite, take your final rest therein. (1:10)

On the doctrine of inaction, see Ch.3.
On not taking possession, not appropriating and not taking credit, see Ch. 51. Identical, or almost identical. lines occur in Chs. 10, 34,51 and 77. Such teachings follow naturally from the realisation of a great, universal, silent, impersonal Tao and from the levelling of all distinctions into One.

3. ACTION WITHOUT DEEDS

Exalt not the wise,[7]
So that the people shall not scheme and contend;
Prize not rare objects,
So that the people shall not steal;
Shut out from sight the things of desire,
So that the people's hearts shall not be disturbed.

Therefore in the government of the Sage:
He keeps empty their hearts[8]
Makes full their bellies,
Discourages their ambitions,
Strengthens their frames;
So that the people may be innocent of knowledge and desires.
And the cunning ones shall not presume to interfere.[9]
By action without deeds
May all live in peace.

7 *Exalting the wise in government is a typically Confucian idea.*
8 *'Empty-heart' in the Chinese language means 'open-mindedness,' or 'humility,' a sign of the cultured gentleman. Sometimes used to mean 'passivity.' Throughout Lao tzu's book, 'empty' and 'full' are used as meaning 'humility' and 'pride' respectively.*
9 *Wei, 'to act,' frequently used in this book to denote 'interfere.' Wu-wei, or 'inaction' practically means non-interference, for it is the exact equivalent of laissez-faire.*

3.1. EXALT NOT THE WISE. A WORLD OF UNCONSCIOUS GOODNESS.

'Was the world at peace when Emperor Shun came to govern it, or was it in chaos and he came to give it an orderly government?' asked Men Wu-kwei.

'If the world had been at peace,' replied Ch'ihchang Manchi, 'the people would have had their wish granted and there would have been no call for Emperor Shun to rule it. He came like a doctor to treat a diseased patient, and the world was like a bald-headed person putting on a toupee, like a sick man seeking a physician. Shun came like a good son who, wearing a sorrowful expression, proffered medicine to a father sick (from neglect),of which the Sage should be ashamed. For in the world of perfect peace, no value was placed upon exalting the wise, or putting the capable men in position. The ruler was like the top of a tree (unconsciously there), and the people lived like the deer of the forest. Doing right, they did not know that it was called justice. Kind to one another, they did not know that it was called humanity. They were straight and did not know it was called faithfulness. They were proper, and did not know it was called honesty. They moved about and called to one another for help, and did not call it favour. Therefore their actions left no trace and their events left no record.' (3:14)

3.2. KNOWLEDGE IS THE INSTRUMENT OF CONTENTION. (CONFUCIUS WAS SPEAKING TO YEN HUEI, HIS DISCIPLE). 'Do your realise how one's character is lost and where knowledge leads?A man loses his character through the desire for fame, and knowledge leads to contention. In the struggle for fame, men crush each other, while their knowledge is but an instrument for scheming and contention. These two are instruments of evil and lead one away from the moral life.'

3.3. HOW THE INCREASE OF KNOWLEDGE AND THE TEACHINGS OF PHILOSOPHERS CORRUPTED THE NATURE OF MAN.

Those who rely upon the arc, the line, compasses, and the square to make correct forms injure the natural constitution of things. Those who use cords to bind and glue to piece together interfere with the natural character of things. Those who seek to satisfy the mind of man by hampering it with ceremonies and music and affecting humanity and justice have lost the original nature of man. There is an original nature in things. Things in their original nature are curved without the help of arcs, straight without lines, round without compasses,and rectangular without squares; they are joined together with-out glue, and hold together without cords. In this manner all things grow with abundant life, without knowing how they do so. They all have a place in the scheme of things without knowing how they come to have their proper place. From time immemorial this has been so, and it may not be tampered with.Why then should the doctrines of humanity and justice continue to remain like so much glue or cords, in the domain of Tao and character, to give rise to confusion and doubt among mankind?

The lesser doubts change man's purpose, and the greater doubts change man's nature. How do we know this? Ever since the time when Shun made a bid for humanity and justice and threw the world into confusion, men have run about and exhausted themselves in the pursuit thereof. Is it not then humanity and justice which have changed the nature of man?

People with superfluous keenness of vision put into confusion the five colours, lose themselves in the forms and designs, and in the distinctions of greens and yellows for sacrificial robes.Is this not so? Of such was Li Chu (the clear-sighted). People with superfluous keenness of hearing put into confusion the five notes, exaggerate the tonic differences of the six pitch-pipes, and the various timbres of metal, stone, string, and bamboo, of the *huang-chung*, and the *ta-lu (Huang-chung and ta-Iu were the standard pitch-pipes)*. Is this not so? Of such was Shih K'uang (the music master). People who abnormally develop humanity, exalt character and suppress nature in order to gain a reputation, make the world noisy with their discussions and cause it to follow impractical doctrines. Is this not so? Of such were Tseng and Shih. People who commit excess in arguments, like piling up bricks and tying knots, analyzing and enquiring into the distinctions of hard and white,identities and differences, wear themselves out over vain, useless terms. Is this not so? Of such were Yang and Mo. All these are superfluous and devious growths of knowledge and are not the correct guide for the world.

He who would be the ultimate guide of the world should take care to preserve the original nature of man. Therefore,with him, the united is not like joined toes, the separated is not like extra fingers, what is long is not considered as excess, and what is short is not regarded as wanting. For duck's legs,though short, cannot be lengthened without dismay to the duck, and a crane's legs, though long, cannot be shortened without misery to the crane. That which is long in nature must not be cut off, and that which is short in nature must not be lengthened. One should not worry about changing them. It would seem that humanity and justice were not part of the nature of man! How worried these teachers of charity are!....

Now the charitable men of the present age go about with a look of concern, sorrowing over the ills of the age, while the non-charitable let loose the desires of their nature in their greed for position and wealth. Therefore it would seem that humanity and justice were not a part of human nature! Yet from the time of the Three Dynasties downwards what a commotion has been raised about them! (3:1, 2)

3.4. THE DOCTRINE OF INACTION (LAISSEZ-FAIRE, NON-INTER-FERENCE), SEEN AS A TEACHING TO ALLOW THE PEOPLE TO 'FULFIL PEACEFULLY THE NATURAL INSTINCTS OF LIFE.' There has been such a thing as letting mankind alone and tolerance; there has never been such a thing as governing mankind. Letting alone springs from the fear lest men's natural dispositions be perverted, and tolerance springs from the fear lest their character be corrupted. But if their natural dispositions be not perverted, nor their character corrupted, what need is there left for government?
Of old, when Yao governed the empire, he made the people live happily; consequently the people struggled to be happy and became restless. When Chieh governed the empire he made the people live in misery; consequently the people regarded life as a burden and were discontented. Restlessness and discontent are subversive of man's character; and without character there has never been such a thing as stability.

When man rejoices greatly, he gravitates towards *yang* (the positive pole). When he is in great anger, he gravitates towards *yin* (the negative pole). When the equilibrium of positive and negative is disturbed, the four seasons are upset, and the balance of heat and cold is destroyed. Man himself suffers physically thereby. It causes men to rejoice and sorrow inordinately, to live disorderly lives, be vexed in their thoughts, and lose their pattern and norm of conduct. When that happens, then the whole world seethes with revolt and discontent, and we have such men as Robber Cheh (and the Confucian teachers), Tseng and Shih. Offer the entire world as rewards for the good or threaten the wicked with the dire punishments of the entire world, and it is still insufficient (to reform them). Consequently, with the entire world, one cannot furnish sufficient inducements or deterrents to action. From the Three Dynasties downwards, the world has lived in a helter-skelter of promotions and punishments. What chance have the people left for fulfilling peacefully the natural instincts of their lives?....
Therefore, when a gentleman is unavoidably compelled to take charge of the government of the empire, there is nothing better than inaction (letting alone). By means of inaction only can he allow the people to fulfil peacefully the natural instincts of their lives. Therefore he who values the world as his own self may be entrusted with the government of the world; and he who loves the world as his own self may be entrusted with the care of the world. Therefore if the gentleman can refrain from disturbing the internal economy of man and glorifying the powers of sight and hearing, he can sit still like a corpse or spring into action like a dragon, be silent as the deep or talk with the voice of thunder, the movements of his spirit calling forth the natural mechanism of Heaven. He can remain calm and leisurely doing nothing, while all things are brought to maturity and thrive. What need then would have I to set about governing the world?(3:6)

The doctrine of inaction as imitation of Tao is developed in 6.1 and in 37.1.

4. THE CHARACTER OF TAO

Tao is a hollow vessel
   And its use is inexhaustible!
Fathomless!
   Like the fountain head of all things
   Its sharp edges rounded off,
   Its tangles untied
   Its light tempered,
   Its turmoil submerged,
Yet dark like deep water it seems to remain.
   I do not know whose Son it is,
   An image of what existed before God.

5. NATURE

Nature is unkind:
   It treats the creation like sacrificial straw-dogs.
The Sage is unkind:
   He treats the people like sacrificial straw-dogs.[10]
How the universe is like a bellows!
   Empty, yet it gives a supply that never fails;
   The more it is worked, the more it brings forth.
By many words is wit exhausted.
Rather, therefore, hold to the core.[11]

  10 *The doctrine of naturalism, the Sage reaching the impartiality and often the stolid difference of Nature.*
  11 *Centre, the original nature of man. "Hold to the core' is an important Taoist tenet.*

6. THE SPIRIT OF THE VALLEY

The Spirit of the Valley[12] never dies.
It is called the Mystic Female.[13]
   The Door of the Mystic Female
   Is the root of Heaven and Earth.

Continuously, continuously,
It seems to remain.
   Draw upon it

And it serves you with ease.[14]

12 The Valley, like the bellows, is a symbol of Taoistic 'emptiness.'
13 The principle of yin, the negative, the receptive, the quiescent.
14 He who makes use of nature's laws accomplishes results 'without labour.'

Below is the first description of the character of Tao as a silent, mystic, life-giving force, as told in an imaginary conversation between Lao tzu and Confucius. The passage also mentions the principle of reversion in an eternal cycle which is basic in Lao tzu's and Chuang tzu's thinking.

4.1. TAO IS LIKE THE SEA.
'We have a little time today,' said Confucius to Lao tzu. 'May I ask what is the great Tao?'
   Lao tzu replied, 'Give a ceremonial bath to your mind! Cleanse your spirit! Throw away your sage wisdom! Tao is dark and elusive, difficult to describe. However, I will outline it for you. Light comes from darkness, and the predicable come from the formless. Life energy comes from Tao, and bodily form is come from life energy, and thus all things of the creation evolve into different forms. Therefore the animals with nine external cavities reproduce by suckling their young, and those with eight cavities reproduce by hatching eggs. Life springs into existence without a visible source and disappears into infinity. It stands in the middle of a vast expanse, without visible exit, entrance or

shelter. He who follows Tao is strong of body, clear of mind and sharp of sight and hearing. He does not clutter up his mind with worries, and is flexible in his adjustment to external conditions. The heaven cannot help being high, the earth cannot help being wide, the sun and the moon cannot help going round, and all things of the creation cannot help but live and grow. Perhaps this is Tao. Besides, the learned is not necessarily wise, and the good talker is not necessarily clever. The Sage eschews these things. But that which is added to and does not increase, is taken away from and does not decrease-that is what the Sage is anxious to preserve. Fathomless, it is like the sea. Awe-inspiring, the cycle begins again when it ends. It sustains all creation and is never exhausted. In comparison with this, the teachings of the gentlemen deal with the superficial externals. What gives life to all creation and is itself inexhaustible-that is Tao.'

'Its sharp edges rounded off, is tangles untied, etc.' These lines are repeated in Ch. 52 and 56. See 56.

"Nature is unkind," 'The Sage is unkind'- These rather puzzling statements are made clear by Chuang tzu in several passages. It should be explained that
(1) Lao tzu has a consistent view of a great Tao,the source of all creation, which rises above all individual things and persons. One of the most important concepts about Tao is that it is entirely impersonal and impartial in its workings. This constitutes one of the most important differences between Tao and the Christian God. In this concept of impartiality, Tao resembles the scientist's concept of an impersonal law, which makes no exceptions for individuals.
(2) Both Chuang tzu and Lao tzu emphasise that Tao benefits all without conscious kindness. In Chuang tzu, the Confucian doctrine of jen ('humanity') is constantly under attack as being a doctrine leading to conscious affectation. In the world of unconscious goodness, the people were 'kind,' but they `did not know it was called humanity';they did right, but `did not know it was called justice' (see 3.1).
(3) Chuang tzu emphasises that the true love of mankind exceeds the Confucian partial love of one's relatives.

5.1. NATURE IS UNKIND. THE SAGE IS UNKIND

(Hsu Yu was describing Tao as his master.) 'Ah! my Master, my Master! He trims down all created things, and does not account it justice. He causes all created things to thrive and does not account it kindness. Dating back further than the remotest antiquity, He does not account himself old. Covering heaven, supporting earth, and fashioning the various forms of things, He does not account himself skilled. It is He whom you should seek.' (2:9)

And so it is that when the Sage wages war, he can destroy a kingdom and yet does not lose the affection of its people; he spreads blessings upon all things, but does not regard it as love of fellowmen..... He who has personal attachments is not humane.

Now perfect Tao cannot be given a name. A perfect argument does not employ words. Perfect Kindness does not concern itself with (individual acts of) kindness. ... For the Tao which is manifest is not Tao. Speech which argues falls short of its aim. Kindness which has fixed objects loses its scope. ...'(1:8)
Prime Minister Tang of Shang asked Chuang tzu about love.
'Tigers and wolves are loving animals,' said Chuang tzu.
'What do you mean?'
'The tiger loves his cub. Why isn't he a loving animal?'
'What about perfect kindness?' asked the prime minister
'Perfect kindness has no regard for particular relations.'
'I have heard it said,' replied Tang, 'that without relations, one has no love, and without love, one has no filial piety. How can you say that the perfectly kind man has no filial piety?'
'You don't understand,' said Chuang tzu. "Perfect kindness is indeed the ideal. It is so much higher than filial piety. The filial piety that you speak of is not enough; it falls short of (true) filial piety.'(4:5)

To a person who is born beautiful people give a mirror. But if people did not tell him, he would not know that he was beautiful. He seems to be aware and yet unaware of it, to have heard and yet not to have heard. Thus he never loses his beauty and people admire him for ever. To a Sage who loves his fellow-men, people give a name (humanity). But if people did not tell him, he would not know that he was kind. He seems to be aware and yet unaware of his kindness, to have heard it and yet not to have heard it. Thus he never loses his kindness, and people are at ease in his presence for ever. (7:1)

5.2. TAO IS LIKE A BELLOWS. Chuang tzu says, 'Tao is deep and profound in its state of rest, crystal clear like a pond. ..Mightily it springs into life, suddenly it moves, and all creation follows. . .. Looked at, it is dark. Listened to, it is noiseless.But in that darkness there appears a light; and in the silence, a harmony is heard.'(3:10)

To be poured into without becoming full, and to pour into without becoming empty, without knowing how this come about-this is the art of preserving the Light. (1:8)

6.1. THE SILENT BEAUTIFUL UNIVERSE. THE 'ROOT' OF ALL THINGS. There is great beauty in the silent universe. There are manifest laws governing the four seasons without words.There is an intrinsic principle in the created things which is not expressed. The Sage looks back to the beauty of the universe and penetrates into the intrinsic principle of created things.

Therefore the perfect man does nothing, the great Sage takes no action. In doing this, he follows the pattern of the universe. The spirit of the universe is subtle and informs all life. Things live and die and change their forms, without knowing the root from which they come. Abundantly it multiplies; eternally it stands by itself. The greatest reaches of space do not leave its confines, and the smallest down of a bird in autumn awaits its power to assume form. The things emerge and submerge, but it remains for ever without change. The *yin* and the *yang* and the four seasons move in orderly procession. Darkly and with.out visible form it seems not to exist and yet exists. The thing of the creation are nourished by it, without knowing it. This is the root, from which one may survey the universe. (6:1)

At this point, it may be stated that most of the teachings about the character of Tao have been covered. Tao is the mother of all things; it cannot be named or predicated; it manifests itself in form and disappears again in formlessness; it does not act; it dose not talk; it is the fathomless and inexhaustible source of all life; it is strictly impersonal. In addition, it is impartial, see Ch. 7; it is immanent, see34.2; and it operates in cycles by the principle of reversion, see Ch. 40,which causes the levelling of all opposites, making alike success and failure, strength and weakness, life and death, etc. From this spring all of Lao tzu's paradoxes.

BOOK TWO

THE LESSONS OF TAO

7. LIVING FOR OTHERS

The universe is everlasting.
The reason the universe is everlasting
   Is that it does not live for Self.[1]
Therefore it can long endure.

Therefore the Sage puts himself last,
   And finds himself in the foremost place;
Regards his body as accidental,
   And his body is thereby preserved.
Is it not because he does not live for Self
That his Self is realised?

1 *Gives life to others through its transformations.*

7.1. THE IMPARTIALITY OF TAO. ANOTHER REASON FOR INACTION.
'What is meant by the phrase "a canton says?"' asked Little Knowledge of T'aikung Tiao.

'A canton,' replied T'aikung Tiao, 'consists of a community of people of different clans and families who are bound together by common customs. It is a community of different units which, when dispersed, become different again. If you take the different parts of a horse separately, you do not get a horse. But a horse surely stands there, by which we mean an animal which comes into being through the combination of the different parts of the horse's body. Therefore, little hillocks pile them-selves up and become a mountain; streams flow into one another and become a great river. The great man unites all things and becomes impartial. Hence it is that (as in the case of an animal) response to external surroundings is guided by a central self which disregards the individual parts, and its own initiative is dictated by a common standard without disparagement. The four seasons are different in temperature not by the individual decisions of heaven; thus it is possible to have a complete year. The officials of the five departments have different duties conferred impartially by the ruler; thus it is possible to have a unified nation. The military and the civilian (who have different talents) are not arbitrarily given office; thus it is possible to have unified morale. The things of the creation have different constitutions, given impartially by Tao; therefore Tao cannot be named. Because it cannot be named (predicated), therefore Tao does not 'do things'; and because it does not 'do things', everything is done. There is a before and an after in time, and the world is in continual change. Fortune and misfortune follow one another; there is some good in what at first displeases. (People) usually look at things from their respective points of view, and miss the truth by wanting to correct others. (Tao) may be compared to a great swamp where timber of all kinds is grown. Look at a great mountain; it tolerates trees and rocks on the same slope. This is what is meant by the phrase "a canton says." '(7:4)

7.2. HEAVEN COVERS AII EQUALLY. Heaven covers all equally. Earth supports all equally. (2:10)

7.3. THE SAGH IS IMPARTIAL. The Master says, 'Great is Tao ! It canopies and sustains all creation. The gentleman cannot but purge his mind (of personal notions and desires). To act by not acting is called heaven. To express without expression is called character. To love one's fellowmen and benefit all is called humanity. To regard the different things as belonging in common is called great. Not to distinguish oneself by conspicuous behaviour is called width of character. To possess diversity is called wealth. Therefore to preserve one's character is called self-discipline. To have one's character developed is to have power.

To follow the Tao is called being complete. Not to allow external events to injure one's mind is called whole. When a gentleman understands these ten (statements), then he achieves greatness of mind and all things converge towards him like a flowing stream. In this case, he leaves the gold in the mountains and leaves the pearls in the sea. He does not place value upon material goods, and he keeps away from honour and wealth. He does not rejoice over long life, nor is he sorry to die young. He does not regard a high position as honour, nor is he ashamed of poverty and failure. He does not set his mind on the wealth of the world and appropriate it for his own benefit. He does not consider ruling the world as his personal glory, and when he is in a position of eminence, he regard the world as one common family. To him life and death are different aspects of the same thing.'(3:10)

8.WATER

The best of men is like water;
    Water benefits all things
    And does not compete with them.
It dwells in (the lowly) places that all disdain.
    Wherein it comes near to the Tao.

In his dwelling, (the Sage) loves the (lowly) earth;
In his heart, he loves what is profound;

In his relations with others, he loves kindness;
In his words, he loves sincerity;
In government, he loves peace;
In business affairs, he love ability;
In his actions, he loves choosing the right time.
   It is because he does not contend
   That he is without reproach.

In a comparative study of Lao tzu and Chuang tzu, probably the most marked difference is that regarding the subject of non-contention As has been pointed out in the preface, the most important and characteristic teaching of Lao tzu is on non-contention, humility, gentility and seeking the lowly position, of which water is the symbol Lao tzu had more passages on teachings of this kind than on any others topic. But is difficult, and almost impossible, to find parallel sayings of Chuang tzu on the same subject. This leads one to think that Chuang tzu was probably a stronger and harder spirit than the mellow master, who emphasized the spirit of the female. Whereas water became for Lao tzu a symbol of the strength of gentleness and the wisdom of lying low, in Chuang tzu, it became the symbol rather of tranquility of spirit. See the preface.

8.1. WATER AS THE SYMBOL OF HEAVENLY VIRTUE. When the body is kept bustling about without stop, it becomes fatigued. When the mind is overworked without stop, it becomes worried, and worry causes exhaustion. The nature of water is that it becomes clear when left alone and becomes still when undisturbed. When it is bottled up and cannot flow, it also cannot remain clear. It is the symbol of heavenly virtue. (4:9)

   Calm represents the nature of water at its best. In that it may serve as our model, for its power is preserved and is not dispersed through agitation. (2:3)

Chuang tzu distinguishes between living on the spiritual and the material level. Although his most characteristic teaching was to allow the human spirit to roam about in the immaterial world, he recognized the necessity of living in this world as we find it and meeting the daily problems of life. The daily problems of living were 'something which could not be helped, and the cannot-be-helped attitude is the attitude of the Sage.' This attitude may be described as one of patient condescension.

8.2. THE TAO OF GOD AND THE TAO OF MAN. That which is low, but must be let alone, is matter. That which is humble, but still must be followed, is the people. That which is always there but still has to be attended to, is affairs. That which is inadequate, but still has to be set forth, is the law. That which is remote from Tao, but still claims our attention, is duty. That which is biased, but must be broadened, is charity. Trivial, but requiring to be strengthened from within, that is ceremony.Contained within, but requiring to be uplifted, that is character. One, but not to be without modification, that is Tao. Spiritual,yet not to be devoid of action, that is God.

Therefore the Sage looks up to God, but does not offer to aid. He perfects his character, but does not involve himself. He guides himself by Tao, but makes no plans. He identifies himself with charity, but does not rely on it. He performs his duties towards his neighbors, but does not set store by them. He responds to ceremony, without avoiding it. He undertakes affairs without declining them, and metes out law without confusion. He relies on the people and does not make light of them. He accommodates himself to the material world and does not ignore it. Things are not worth attending to, yet they have to be attended to. He who does not understand God will not be pure in character. He who has not clear apprehension of Tao will not know where to begin. And he who is not enlightened by Tao-alas indeed for him!

What then is Tao? There is the Tao of God, and there is the Tao of man. Honour through inaction comes from the Tao of God: entanglement through action comes from the Tao of man. The Tao of God is fundamental: the Tao of man is accidental. The distance which separates them is great. Let us all take heed thereto! (3:9)

To adjust oneself to events and surroundings casually is the way of Tao. (6:3)

9. THE DANGER OF OVERWEENING SUCCESS

Stretch (a bow) to the very full,
   And you will wish you had stopped in time.
Temper a (sword-edge) to its very sharpest,
   And the edge will not last long.
When gold and jade fill your hall,
   You will not be able to keep them safe.
To be proud with wealth and honour
   Is to sow the seeds of one's own downfall.
Retire when your work is done,
   Such is Heaven's way.[2]

2 *The whole chapter is rhymed.*

9.1. THE SMUGS, THE SNUGS AND THE HUMPBACK. There are smugs, there are snugs and there are humpbacks. Smugs are those people who having heard what their teacher says, feel very, very satisfied and very pleased with themselves. They think they have learned the truth and do not realize that there was a time when no material universe existed. The snugs are lice on the bodies of hogs. They choose their abode in the long mane and hair of the hogs and believe themselves to be living in a grand palace with a big garden. They hide themselves in the corners, armpits, breasts and legs of the pigs and think that they are living in security. They do not realize that one day the butcher may come and rolling up his sleeve begin to lay hay under it and set fire to singe the pig, and both themselves and the pig will be scorched to death. This is to live within the limitations of their own choice. These are the snugs. The humpback was Emperor Shun. The mutton does not crave for the ants but the ants crave for mutton because of its rank smell. Because Emperor Shun had a rank character which attracted the people, the people loved him. Therefore, after he changed his capital three times and had moved to the plains of Teng, there were over a hundred thousand people who followed him. Emperor Yao heard of Shun's ability and put him in charge of a barren district, saying, 'I hope that people who follow him there will receive the benefit of his rule' When Shun was put in charge of the barren district, he was already growing old, his eyesight and hearing were failing, but he was not allowed to retire. This is what I call a humpback.

9.2. THE DANGERS OF HOARDING WEALTH.
Mankouteh says, 'The shameless become rich and the good talkers become high officials.'(8:7)

9.3. A Group of Confucians were digging up a grave in the hope of finding old manuscripts. The leader among them said, 'It is already dawn. Have we finished?'

'No,' replied the little Confucians, 'we haven't yet stripped the dead man's clothes, and we know that he keeps a pearl in his mouth. There is an old verse which says, "How green is the wheat! It grows on the hillsides. He did not give money to the poor when he was living, why did he carry a pearl in his mouth when he died?"

The group of Confucians therefore smashed in the dead man's temples, pulled his whiskers and, taking a metal hammer to knock open his jaw, they gradually tore open his cheek. But they were careful not to hurt the pearl in the dead man's mouth. (7:6)

9.4. INSCRIPTION ON HUMILITY. Chengk'aofu (the tenth-generation ancestor of Confucius) left the following inscription: 'On my first promotion, I bent my head. On my second promotion, I bent from my waist. On my third promotion, I prostrated myself. I walked close to the walls on the side of the street and no one dared to insult me.' As for the common men: they begin to swagger on their first promotion. On their second promotion, they begin to dance on the wagon. On their third promotion, they begin to call themselves the elders. (8:14)

9.5. THE STORY OF BUTCHER YUEH. When King Chao of Ch'u had to flee his country, the lamb butcher Yueh also ran away and became a follower of the king. When the king returned to his country, he was going to reward those who had followed him in his exile. When it came the butcher's turn, he said, 'When His Majesty lost his kingdom, I lost my butcher' business. Now His Majesty has recovered his kingdom and I have returned to be a butcher. I have already regained what I lost. I do not need any reward.' The king still insisted and the butcher said, 'when His Majesty lost his kingdom, I had nothing to do with it; therefore I did not deserve punishment. Now His Majesty has returned, it has nothing to do with me; therefore I dare not ask for reward.' The king still summoned him to appear in his presence and the butcher refused, saying, 'According to the laws of the kingdom, only one who has rendered a great service to his country is entitled to seeing the king. I had neither the wisdom to preserve the kingdom nor the bravery to die in its defence. When the Wu Army entered the capital, I was just scared and ran away. I did not mean to follow His Majesty. Now His Majesty wishes to make an exception and asks to see me. I hardly think that is the proper thing to do at all'. (8:2)

This selection is from Chapter 28, which is generally regarded as spurious.

10. EMBRACING THE ONE

In embracing the One[3] with your soul,
    Can you never forsake the Tao?
In controlling your vital force to achieve gentleness,
    Can you become like the new-born child?[4]
In cleansing and purifying your Mystic vision,
    Can you strive after perfection?
In loving the people and governing the kingdom,
    Can you rule without interference?
In opening and shutting the Gate of Heaven,
    Can you play the part of the Female?[5]

In comprehending all knowledge,
    Can you renounce the mind?[6]

To give birth, to nourish,
To give birth without taking possession,
To act without appropriation.
To be chief among men without managing them-
This is the Mystic Virtue.

3 Important phrase in Taoism
4 The babe as symbol of innocence, a common imagery found also in Chuang tzu sometimes the imagery of the "new-born calf" is used
5 The Yin, the receptive, the passive, the quiet. "The Door of the Mystic Female is the root of heaven and earth, see Ch. 6
6 This section is rhymed throughout.

Chuang tzu reports a conversation of Lao tzu which in all essential points agrees with the teachings of this chapter.

10.1. LAO TZU ON MENTAL HYGIENE.

Nanyungch'u brought along his food and travelled for seven days and nights and arrived at Lao tzu's place.

    Do you come from Ch'u?

    'Yes.' replied Nanyungch'u

    'Why do you come with such a big crowd?' said Lao tzu. Nanyungch'u's face changed and he looked behind him, and Lao tzu said to him, 'I suppose you don't understand what I mean.'

    Nanyungch'u bent his head, embarrassed, and he lifted his head and said with a sigh, 'I didn't know how to reply to your question. And now I have even forgotten what I came to ask you about.'

    'What is on your mind?' said Lao tzu.

    'The trouble with me,' said Nanyungch'u, 'is that if I do not learn knowledge, people call me a fool. And if I learn knowledge, it makes me so sad. If I do not learn kindness, I injure others, and if I learn kindness, I become worried (for others). If I do not learn justice, I do harm to others, and if I learn justice, I cause sorrow to myself. How can I escape this dilemma? These three things worry me. That is why I have come to ask you.'

'I saw something in your eyes a moment ago,' said Lao tzu,' and I knew your trouble already. Now you have told me exactly what I thought. You look as if you have lost your parents or like one who goes out with a bamboo pole to fathom the sea. Indeed, you are a lost soul! You wish to recover your original nature, but you are confused and do not know where to begin. I am so sorry for you.'

Nanyungch'u asked to withdraw and he began to ponder over what he wanted and dismiss his fears and worries. He sat in his room alone and sorrowful for ten days. After that, he came to see Lao tzu again.

'You have given yourself a bath,' said Lao tzu, 'and the dirt seems to have come off with the hot steam, but something still circulates inside. When you are disturbed by the external senses and worried and confused, you should rest your mind and seek tranquility inside. When your mind is blocked and gets beyond your control, then you should shut out your external senses. Those who are disturbed by their senses and their minds cannot preserve their own character. How much less can they follow the Tao!'

'A man is sick,' said Nanyungch'u, 'and his neighbour comes to visit him. The patient can tell his neighbour about his sickness, but the visitor who comes to see the sick man is not sick himself. What I have heard about the Tao is like taking medicine which increases my sickness. Can you tell me the principles of mental hygiene?'

'The principles of mental hygiene are as follows,' said Lao tzu. 'Can you embrace the One? Can you never forsake the Tao? Can you divine fortune and misfortune without the help of soothsayers? Do you know where to stop? Can you let unimportant things go? Can you learn not to depend on others but to seek it in yourself? Can you come and go unfettered inspirit and can you purge your mind of knowledge? Can you be (innocent) like a new-born child? The baby cries all day and yet his voice never becomes hoarse; that is because he has not lost nature's harmony. The baby clenches his hands all day without holding anything; that is because he is following his original character. The baby looks at things all day without winking; that is because his eyes are not focused on any particular object. He goes without knowing where he is going, and stops without knowing what he is doing. He merges himself with the surroundings and moves along with it. These are the principles of mental hygiene.' (6:7)

Lao tzu uses the child, as he uses the 'uncarved wood,' as a symbol of the whole, unspoiled nature of man.

10.2. THE SONS OF HEAVEN AND THE SONS OF MEN. Those who are straight inside (follow their original instincts) are the sons of Heaven. The sons of Heaven know that both themselves and the emperor are equally sons of Heaven..... Such people are called children. This is what is meant by 'sons of Heaven.'
Those who bend outwards (follow customs and conventions) are sons of men. They bow and they kneel down and they clasp their hands in greeting. Such is the ceremony of a ruler's subjects. All people do it. How would I dare to be an exception? To do what the others do and not be criticized by others, this is to be the sons of men.

'To give birth, to nourish', etc. See identical lines and interpretation-in Ch.51.

11. THE UTILITY OF NOT-BEING

Thirty spokes unite around the nave;
   From their not-being (loss of their individuality)
   Arises the utility of the wheel.
Mould clay into a vessel;
   From its not-being (in the vessel's hollow)
   Arises the utility of the vessel.
Cut out doors and windows in the house (-wall),
   From their not-being (empty space) arises the utility of the house.
Therefore by the existence of things we profit.
And by the non-existence of things we are served.

11.1. THE USEFULNESS OF NOT-BEING. When the eye is cleared of obstacles it sees sharply. When the ear is cleared of obstacles it hears well. When the nose is not blocked up, it smells well. When the mouth is cleared, it tastes well. When the mind is clear, it thinks well. When knowledge is cleared of obstacles, one attains the character of Tao. Tao must not be blocked: when it is blocked it is choked and if it continues to be choked, it stumbles. When it stumbles, all creation is harmed. All sentient life depends on the breath. When the breath is disturbed, it is not the fault of nature. Nature keeps it open day and night without cease, but man continuously blocks it up. The human embryo has a surrounding membrane (which allows it to move about), and the human mind must be free to roam about in the universe. When there is no empty space in a house, then the mother-in-law and daughter-in-law bicker with one another. When the mind is deprived of its opportunity to roam about, then the six instincts begin to clash with one another. The reason why we feel good when going to a great forest or a hill is because our spirits are usually cramped.(7:8)

11.2. THE USE OF USELESSNESS
'You always speak of (the use of) uselessness,' said Hueitse to Chuang tzu

'One must understand the use of uselessness before he can speak of the use of usefulness. Surely, the earth is vast and great yet what man can put to use is only where his feet rest. However, when a man turns up his toe and his body is laid in the grave, can he still find the earth useful?'
'Then the earth is useless to him,' replied Hucitse.
"Is it not clear, therefore, that the useless (grave) is useful(because of the hollow or the non-existence of the earth)?"
 A man walks upon the ground by stepping on it, but it is only through the ground that he does not step upon (the distance between the steps) that he is able to reach a great distance.

11.3. THE COMFORT OF UNAWARENESS. A good craftsman draws lines and circles without the help of compasses and squares. His fingers are so sensitively attuned to his material that he does not depend on the direction of his mind. Therefore, his mind remains unfettered. Unawareness of one's feet is the mark of a pair of shoes that fit; unawareness of the waist is the sign of a belt that fits; unawareness of right and wrong is the mark of a mind that is at ease. It does not change inside and is not affected by external events, and one feels at ease in all circumstances and situations. Once at ease, it is never again not at ease. That is to be at ease through unawareness of being at ease. (5:7)

For an illustration of the usefulness of a useless tree, see selection 22.3.

12. THE SENSES
The five colours blind the eyes of man;
The five musical notes deafen the ears of man;
The five flavours dull the taste of man;
Horse-racing, hunting and chasing madden the minds of man;
Rare, valuable goods keep their owners awake at night.[7]

Therefore the Sage:

Provides for the belly and not for the eye.[8]
Hence, he rejects the one and accepts the other.

7 Lit "Keep one on one's guard.
8 "Belly' here refers to the inner self, the unconscious, the instinctive; the 'eye' refers to the external self or the sensuous world.

12.1. THE FIVE SENSES DETRACT FROM OUR NATURE.

There are five ways in which we lose our original nature. First, the five colors confuse the eye and obstruct our vision. Second, the five notes confuse the ear and obstruct our hearing. Third. the five smells assail our nostrils and block up our forehead. Fourth, the five tastes foul the mouth and hurt our taste. Fifth, desires and occupations confuse our mind and cause agitation of our spirit. All these do injury to our life, and yet Yang Chu and Motse regard them as (means towards) fulfilment. That is not what I would regard as fulfilment. For if fulfilment means enslavement, how can it be regarded as fulfilment? If so, then the pigeon and the owl in a cage may regard themselves as having fulfilled themselves. Besides, if a man's mind is cluttered with desires and occupations and his body is enclosed in a fur cap, or a kingfisher hat, and belts and ceremonial tablets. His mind a mass of stuffed confusion inside and his body a bundle of entanglements outside, and he still claims self-fulfilment from behind that bundle of entanglements, then the convict whose hands are tied behind his back and whose fingers are in a squeezer, and the tigers and leopards behind the bars, may also claim fulfilment of their nature. (3:15)

12.2. ACTION OF THE WIND ON WATER. When a wind passes over the river, it takes away something from the river. When the sun shines on the river, it also takes away something from the river. Yet if you ask the wind and the sun to keep on acting on the river, the river is not conscious of its loss because it is fed by a living source. Such is the gradual, intimate action of water upon the earth, the gradual, intimate relation between shadow and substance and the gradual, intimate action of material things upon other things. Therefore the eye is harmful to (the innate capacity of) vision, the ear is harmful to (the innate capacity of) hearing, and the mind is harmful to (the innate capacity of) understanding. All functions are harmful to their respective organs. When the harm is done, it is beyond repair, for such effect accumulate and grow. (6:16)

12.3. DISTRACTIONS OF THE MATERIAL WORLD.
From the Three Dynasties downwards (since human civilization began), there is no man but has changed his nature on account of material things. The common men sacrifice their lives for profit; the scholars sacrifice their lives for fame; the noblemen sacrifice their lives for their families; the Sage sacrifices his life for the world. All these people have different professions and their reputations vary, but in suffering injury to their original nature, they are alike. Two shepherds, Tsang and Ku, were both tending their sheep and both lost them. On being asked what he was doing, Tsang replied that he was reading with the shepherd's stick under his arm. On being asked what he was doing, Ku replied that he was gambling. The manner in which the two lost their sheep was different, but the fact of their losing their sheep was the same.(3:2)

13. PRAISE AND BLAME
'Favour and disgrace cause one dismay;
What we value and what we fear are within our Self'

What does this mean:

'Favour and disgrace cause one dismay?'
Those who receive a favour from above
Are dismayed when they receive it,
And dismayed when they lose it.

What does this mean:
'What we value and what we fear are within our Self?'
We have fears because we have a self.
When we do not regard that self as self.
What have we to fear?

Therefore he who values the world as his self
May then be entrusted with the government of the world;
And he who loves the world as his self-
The world may then be entrusted to his care.

Man's loss of his original nature comes from the distractions of the material world acting through the five senses. His emancipation of the spirit comes from the doctrine of selflessness which appears to be the common ideal of sainthood in all religions. n Taoist philosophy, this emancipation through selflessness comes through the realization that the individual self is nothing and the great unity of the universe is everything. From this selfless point of view it is therefore natural to regard all the accidents of fortune and misfortune, of honour and disgrace, as things that are entirely superficial and unimportant.

The entire line 'Therefore he who values the world as his self may then be entrusted with the government of the world; and he who loves the world as his self-the world may then been trusted to his care' *appears in Chuang tzu in identical wording in selection 3.4, where the context makes the meaning clear.*

13.1. DEFINITION OF HONOUR AND HAPPINESS.

When one is strong in the knowledge of Tao, one disregards the petty problems of life; when one is strong in the knowledge of character, one ignores the petty problems of knowledge. Petty knowledge is injurious to one's character, and petty conduct is injurious to Tao. Therefore, it is said. 'All that one needs to do is to return to the norm himself.'

Perfect happiness is described as success. When the ancients spoke of success, they did not mean the symbols of rank and honour; they meant by success the state wherein one's happiness was complete. The modern man means by success the badges of rank and honour. But the badges of rank and honour on a man's body have nothing to do with his original self. They are things that are accidentally loaned to him for a period. You cannot refuse them when they are loaned to you, nor can you keep them when they are taken away from you. Therefore, one should not forget oneself over such insignia of authority, nor should one do what the world is doing because of failure and poverty. He is happy in failure as well as in success, and, therefore, he is without sorrow. If a man is unhappy because things loaned to him have been taken away from him, then it is clear that when he was happy, he had lost his true self. There-fore, it is said, 'Those who lose their selves in material things and lose their original nature in the material world may be compared to people who stand on their heads.'(4:10)

13.2. OWNERSHIP

'Can one obtain Tao and possess it?' asked Emperor Shun of Ch'en.

'You don't even own your self. How can you possess Tao?'

'If I don't possess my self, who possesses it?'

'Yourself,' replied Ch'en, 'is a body lent to you by the universe. Your life is not possessed by you; it is a harmony lent to you by the universe. Your nature is not possessed by you; it is a natural evolution lent to you by the universe. Your children and grandchildren are not possessed by you; they are the thrown-off skins (as of snakes or cicadas) lent to you by the universe. Therefore, one goes about without knowing where he is going, stops without knowing what he is holding on to, and eats without knowing how the food tastes. Such activities are merely the working of the *yang* principle of the universe when it is in dominance. How can you ever possess (Tao)?' (6:2)

From this general point of view, the Taoist develops the teachings that 'the perfect man is selfless,' that instead of seeking security in a special corner of one's home and family, one should rather 'entrust that which belongs to the universe to the whole universe,' and, therefore, 'men should lose themselves in Tao as fish lose themselves in water.'

13.3. THE PERFECT MAN IS SELFLESS.

And a lake sparrow laughed, and said: 'Pray, what may that creature be going to do? I rise but a few yards in the air and settle down again, after flying around among the reeds. That is as much as anyone would want to fly. Now, wherever can this creature be going to?'

Such, indeed, is the difference between small and great. Take, for instance, a man who creditably fills some shall office, or whose influence spreads over a village, or whose character pleases a certain prince. His opinion of himself will be much the same as that lake sparrow's. The philosopher Yung of Sung would laugh at such a one. If the whole world flattered him, he would not be affected thereby, nor if the whole world blamed him would he be dissuaded from what he was doing. For Yung can distinguish between essence and superficialities, and understand what is true honour and shame. Such men are rare in their generation. But even he has not established himself.

Now Liehtse[9] could ride upon the wind. Sailing happily in the cool breeze, he would go on for fifteen days before his return. Among mortals who attain happiness, such a man is rare. Yet although Liehtse could dispense with walking, he would still have to depend upon something.[10] As for one who is charioted upon the eternal fitness of Heaven and Earth, driving before him the changing elements as his team to roam through the realms of the Infinite, upon what, then, would such a one have need to depend?

> [9] Philosopher about whose life nothing is known. The book Liehtse is considered a later compilation.
> [10] The wind.

Thus it is said. 'The perfect man ignores self; the divine man ignores achievement; the true Sage ignores reputation.'

The doctrine of the great man is (fluid) as shadow to form, as echo to sound. Ask and it responds, fulfilling its abilities as the help-mate of humanity. Noiseless in repose, objectless in motion, he brings you out of the confusion of your coming and going to wander in the Infinite. Formless in his movements he is eternal with the sun. In respect of his bodily existence, he conforms to the universal standards. Through conformance to the universal standards, he forgets his own individuality. But if he forgets his individuality, how can he regard his possessions as possessions? Those who see possessions in possessions were the wise men of old. Those who regard not possessions as possessions are the friends of Heaven and Earth. (3:9)

13.4. 'ENTRUSTING THAT WHICH BELONGS TO THE UNIVERSE TO THE WHOLE UNIVERSE.' A boat may be hidden in a creek, or concealed in a bog, which is generally considered safe. But at midnight a strong man may come and carry it away on his back. Those dull of understanding do not perceive that how-ever you conceal small things in larger ones, there will always be a chance of losing them. But if you entrust that which belongs to the universe to the whole universe, from it there will be no escape. For this is the great law of things.

To have been cast in this human form is to us already a source of joy. How much greater joy beyond our conception to know that that which is now in human form may undergo countless transitions, with only the infinite to look forward to? Therefore it is that the Sage rejoices in that which can never be lost, but endures always. For if we emulate those who can accept graciously long age or short life and the vicissitudes of events, how much more that which informs all creation on which all changing phenomena depend? (2:6)

BOOK THREE

THE IMITATION OF TAO

14. PREHISTORIC ORIGINS

Looked at, but cannot be seen -
   That is called the Invisible *(yi)*.
Listened to, but cannot be heard-
   That is called the Inaudible *(hsi)*
Grasped at, but cannot be touched.
   That is called the Intangible *(wei)*.[1]
These three elude all our enquiries.
And hence blend and become One.

Not by its rising, is there light,
Nor by it sinking, is there darkness.
   Unceasing, continuous,
    It cannot be defined,
And reverts again to the realm of nothingness.

That is why it is called the Form of the Formless,
The Image of Nothingness.
That is why it is called the Elusive:
    Meet it and you do not see its face;
    Follow it and you do not see its back.

He who holds fast to the Tao of old
    In order to manage the affairs of Now
Is able to know the Primeval Beginnings
    Which are the continuity[2] of Tao.

   1 Jesuit scholars consider these three words (in ancient Chinese pronounced nearly like i-hi-vei) an interesting coincidence with the Hebrew word 'Jahve.'
   2 Chi, a word meaning 'main body of tradition,' 'system' and also 'discipline.'

   The present book is more mystical. One is persuaded to believe that the Tao cannot be named, predicated or described, that it cannot be known. What is left, then, is a feeling of awe and reverence for the mystery and beauty of the universe and its silent, eternal transformations. One has a feeling of despair that Tao is illusive, that it eludes all our enquiries and efforts at discovery, in the same way that some of the deepest and most elementary problems of life evade the biologists. We see how life comes into being, but just as we think we are about to discover its secret, we face a blank. When mystics speak in mysterious terms about the Tao of the universe and is illusiveness, it should be remembered that it is a feeling that is shared not by the mystics alone but by all scientists who think. It is my belief that this reverence for the unknown comes nearest to the religion acceptable to a scientist.

Here, one plunges right into the problem of form and formlessness, of invisible principles of causation, and one is forced to assume a 'root,' an original principle, a source of power, a final cause, which can never be proved or seen or felt or heard. In Taoist philosophy, the only definite things said about Tao are that it neither acts nor talks and that there is a silent procession of changes going round all the time and an eternal cycle of activity and quiescence, of things reverting to their opposites and of material forms appearing and disappearing into infinity. This image of a silent, all-pervasive Tao becomes the model for the Taoist who wishes to keep his original nature and to attain that enormous reserve of power shown by Tao itself. Hence the doctrines of humility, of not claiming credit for one's actions, of calm and quietude, and of forgetting one's individuality in the general processes of change of the fluid universe.

14.1. THE INVISIBLE, INAUDIBLE AND INTANGIBLE.
  'Do you exist or do you not?' asked Light of Nothing.
  Light received no reply and he stared hard at him. Nothing was dark and empty. All day, Light tried to look, but could not see him; listened, but could not hear him; and tried to touch him, but could not find him. 'Alas,' said Light to himself, 'this is the highest limit! Who can attain to such ultimate height! I can be conscious of not-being, but cannot be unconscious of not-being. When I am conscious of not-being, there is still consciousness. How does he ever attain to this height?'(6:4)

14.2. All things come to life, but we cannot see their source. All things appear but we cannot see the gate from which they come. All men value the knowledge of what they know, but really do not know. Only those who fall back upon what knowledge cannot know really know. Is this not a great problem? One must leave it alone and yet one cannot go anywhere without meeting it. This is what (the philosophers) call 'It is so, I think. Or isn't it?'(7:4)

14.3. Looked at, it is without form. Listened to, it is without noise. Men call this the dark and the fathomless. Therefore, the Tao which can be discussed is not Tao. (6:4)

In the following parable, Chuang tzu takes, for example, a succession of things that have relatively less and less form, to illustrate the truth that the formless is the most efficient of all.

14.4. THE PARABLE OF THE ANIMALS, THE WIND AND THE MIND.

The k'uei (a one-legged hopping animal) envies the centipede, the centipede envies the snake, the snake envies the wind, the wind envies the eye, and the eye envies the mind.

'I hop about with one leg,' said k'uei to the centipede.'There is no one who moves about more simply than I do. Now you have so many legs. How do you manage?'

'How do I manage?' replied the centipede. 'Haven't you seen a man spitting? The spittle comes in big drops like beads and small droplets like mist, and they all fall together without number. When I move my natural mechanism, I really don't know how I manage my legs.'

'I move about with so many legs,' said the centipede to the snake. 'How is it that I do not go so fast as you do without legs at all?'

'Each one,' replied the snake, 'moves in his own way by his natural mechanism. What need do I have for legs?'

'I move about with my spine,' said the snake to the wind.'Now, at least I have something like a leg. But you come booming up from the North Sea and booming down to the South Sea, and you seem to have no body. How is that?'

'Indeed,' replied the wind, 'I go booming up from the North Sea and booming down to the South Sea. Yet whoever sticks his finger into me overcomes me, and whoever kicks me also overcomes me. However, only I can tear up big trees and blow off big houses. Therefore, from a great number of small defeats I achieve the great victory. Achieving the great victory belongs to the Sage alone.'(4:13)

Chuang tzu did not complete the parable. But it is evident that he implied that the wind, which is air, envies the eye, because vision or light (which approaches the limit of corpuscular and non-corpuscular existence) travels still faster than the wind. Finally, the mind, which can travel across the centuries of time and leap across the continents of space in the flash of a second and is formless itself, travels even faster than light.

15. THE WISE ONES OF OLD

The wise ones[3] of old had subtle wisdom and depth of understanding;
So profound that they could not be understood.
And because they could not be understood,
Perforce must they be so described:
    Cautious, like crossing a wintry stream,
    Irresolute, like one fearing danger all around,
    Grave, like one acting as guest,
    Self-effacing, like ice beginning to melt,
    Genuine,[4] like a piece of undressed wood,[5]
    Open-minded, like a valley,
    And mixing freely,[6] like murky water.

Who can find repose in a muddy world?
    By lying still, it becomes clear.
Who can maintain his calm for long?
    By activity, it comes back to life.
He who embraces this Tao
    Guards against being over-full,
Because he guards against being over-full,[7]
    He is beyond wearing out and renewal.

3 Another ancient text, the 'rulers.'
4 Tun, 'thickness,' like solid furniture, associated with the original simplicity of man, in opposition to 'thinness,' associated with cunning, over-refinement and sophistication.

5 *P'u, important Taoist idea, the uncarved, the unembellished, the natural goodness and honesty of man. Generally used to mean simplicity, plainness of heart and living.*
6 *Hun, 'muddled,' 'mixing freely,' therefore 'easygoing,' 'not particular.' Taoist wisdom: a wise man should appear like a fool.*
7 *Self-satisfaction, conceit.*

Because the eternal principle of life, Tao, works silently and apparently without action in the way that spring comes round every year, because Tao does not claim credit for its individual acts and is content to be silent, it becomes the image for the Taoist sage.

15.1. THE DEMEANOUR OF THE PURE MAN.
The pure men of old slept without dreams, and waked up without worries. They ate with indifference to flavour, and drew deep breaths. For true men draw breath from their heels; the vulgar only from their throats. Out of the crooked, words are retched up like vomit. When men's attachments are deep, their divine endowments are shallow.

The pure men of old did not know what it was to love life or to hate death. They did not rejoice in birth, nor strive to put off dissolution. Unconcerned they came and unconcerned they went. That was all. They did not forget whence it was they had sprung; neither did they seek to enquire their return thither. Cheerfully they accepted life, waiting patiently for their restoration (the end). This is what is called not to allow the mind to lead one astray from Tao, and not to supplement the natural by human means. Such a one may be called a pure man.

Such men are free in mind and calm in demeanour, with high foreheads. Sometimes disconsolate like autumn, and sometimes warm like spring, their joys and sorrows are in direct touch with the four seasons, in harmony with all creation, and none know the limit thereof ...

The pure men of old appeared of towering stature and yet could not topple down. They behaved as though wanting in themselves, but without looking up to others.

Naturally independent of mind, they were not severe. Living in unconstrained freedom, yet they did not try to show off. They appeared to smile as if pleased, and to move only in natural response to surroundings. Their serenity flowed from the store of goodness within. In social relationships, they kept to their inner character. Broadminded, they appeared great; towering, they seemed beyond control. Continuously abiding, they seemed like doors kept shut; absent-minded, they seemed to forget speech.(2:4)

As seen already in selection 8.I, Chuang tzu uses water as the symbol of spiritual calm which is described as 'the nature of water at its best', and as a symbol of Tao itself which alternates between perfect tranquillity and periodic motion. 'When the body is kept hustling about without stop, it becomes fatigued. When the mind is overworked without stop, it becomes worried, and worry causes exhaustion. The nature of water is that it becomes clear when left alone, and becomes still when undisturbed...it is the symbol of heavenly virtue.'

15.2. CONFUCIUS ON WATER. Confucius says, 'A man cannot see his own image in flowing water but sees it in water which is at rest. Only that which remains at rest itself can become the resting-place for all those which wish to seek rest.'(2:1)

16. KNOWING THE ETERNAL LAW
Attain the utmost in Passivity,
Hold firm to the basis of Quietude.

The myriad things take shape and rise to activity,
   But I watch them fall back to their repose.
Like vegetation that luxuriantly grows
   But returns to the root (soil) from which it springs.

To return to the root is Repose;
   It is called going back to one's Destiny.

Going back to one's Destiny is to find the Eternal Law.[8]
   To know the Eternal Law is Enlightenment.
And not to know the Eternal Law
   Is to court disaster.

He who knows the Eternal Law is tolerant;
Being tolerant, he is impartial;
Being impartial, he is kingly;[9]
Being kingly, he is in accord with Nature;[10]
Being in accord with Nature, he is in accord with Tao;
Being in accord with Tao, he is eternal,
And his whole life is preserved from harm.

8 Ch'ang, the 'constant,' the law of growth and decay, of necessary alternation of opposites, can be interpreted as the 'universal law of nature, or the "inner law of man,'the true self (hsingming chih ch'ang), the two being identical in their nature.
9 Wang; a possible translation is 'cosmopolitan,' i.e, regarding the world as one.
10 T'ien, heaven or nature. Both t'ien here and Tao in the next line are clearly used as adjectives; hence the translation 'in accord with.' T'ien very commonly means 'nature,' or 'natural.'

  The doctrine of passivity ('emptiness') and quietude arises necessarily from the doctrine of reversion. Action or activity is seen as a temporary manifestation of Tao, while quiescence is regarded as the form of Tao reverting to its original form. The doctrine of eternal reversion from activity to inactivity is the basic philosophy of Taoism.It is constantly referred to in many places and amplified in chapters 25,37, and particularly 40.

16.1. THE SAGE USES HIS MIND LIKE A MIRROR. Be not the representative of fame. Make not your mind a clearing-house of plans and strategy. Let things take their natural course, and do not presume to preside over the wise. Understand and trace things to their infinite source and roam about in the sphere beyond the evidences of reality. Fulfil what you have received from heaven and do not hold yourself the possessor thereof. In other words, be passive (as a mirror). The Sage uses his mind like a mirror. It remains in its place passively, and it gives back what it receives without concealment. Therefore it can overcome things without injuring (distorting) them.(2:16)

16.2. CALM AS A COUNTER-AGENT AGAINST NERVOUSNESS. Rest is conducive to a patient's recuperation. Rubbing one's eyes is restful for the man of old age. Tranquillity can cure a man of nervousness. However, all the activities that the busy man is busy about are left alone by the man of leisure. That which the Sage frightens the world with, the divine man leaves alone. That which the wise man frightens the world with, the Sage leaves alone. That which the gentleman frightens the world with, the wise man leaves alone. That which the common men do in order to follow the conventions, the gentleman leaves alone. (7:8)

16.3. 'RETURNING TO THE ROOT.' CONVERSATION BETWEEN GENERAL CLOUDS AND THE GREAT NEBULOUS. When General Clouds was going eastward, he passed through the branches of Fuyao (a magic tree) and happened to meet Great Nebulous. The latter was slapping his thighs and hopping about. When General Clouds saw him, he stopped like one lost and stood still, saying, 'Who are you, old man, and what are you doing here?'
'Strolling!' replied Great Nebulous, still slapping his thighs and hopping about.
　'I want to ask about something,' said General Clouds.
　'Ough!' uttered Great Nebulous.

'The spirits of Heaven are out of harmony,' said General Clouds; 'the spirits of the Earth are smothered; the six influences[11] of the weather do not work together, and the four seasons are no longer regular. I desire to blend the essence of the six influences and nourish all living beings. What am I to do?'

'I do not know! I do not know!' cried Great Nebulous, shaking his head, while still slapping his thighs and hopping about.

So General Clouds did not press his question. Three years later, when passing eastward through the plains of the Sungs, he again fell in with Great Nebulous. The former was overjoyed, and hurrying up, said, 'Has your Holiness[12] forgotten me? Has your Holiness[12] forgotten me?'

He then kowtowed twice and desired to be allowed to interrogate Great Nebulous; but the latter said, 'I wander on without knowing what I want. I rush about without knowing whither I am going. I simply stroll about, watching unexpected events. What should I know?'

'I too regard myself as rushing about,' answered General Clouds; 'but the people follow my movements. I cannot shake the people off and what I do they follow. I would gladly receive some advice.'

'That the scheme of Heaven is in confusion,' said Great Nebulous, 'that the conditions of life are violated, that the will of the Dark Heaven is not accomplished, that the beasts of the field are scattered, that the birds of the air cry at night, that

---

11 *Yin, yang, wind, rain, light and darkness.*
12 *Great Nebulous is here addressed as 'Heaven.'*

blight strikes the trees and herbs, that destruction spread among the creeping things-this, alas! is the fault of those who would rule others.'

'True', replied General Clouds, 'but what am I to do?'

'Ah!' cried Great Nebulous, 'keep quiet and go home in peace!'

'It is not often,' urged General Clouds, 'that I meet with your Holiness. I would gladly receive some advice.

'Ah,' said Great Nebulous, 'nourish your heart. Rest in inaction, and the world will be reformed of itself. Forget your body and spit forth intelligence. Ignore all differences an become one with the Infinite. Release your mind, and free your spirit. Be vacuous, be devoid of soul. Thus will things grow and prosper and return to their Root. Returning to their Root without their knowing it, the result will be a formless whole which will never be cut up. To know it is to cut it up. Ask not about its name, enquire not into its nature, and all things will flourish of themselves.

'Your Holiness.' said General Clouds, 'has informed me with power and taught me silence. What I had long sought, I have now found.' Thereupon he kowtowed twice and took leave.

16.4. THE ORIGIN OF THINGS AND REVERSION TO THE GRAND HARMONY. In the beginning of things, there was a time when even nothing did not exist, and then something came into existence which had no name. From this, One arose but this one did not yet have form. The source from which things come into being is called teh (character, or Tao embodied). Things have not yet received their form, but the division of the yang(positive) and yin (negative) principles which are intimately related to each other already appear-this is called natural constitution. When (the yin and the yang) begin to move,things come into being. When things are formed in accordance with the principles of life-this is called form. When the bodily form shelters the spirit where each part behaves according to its own pattern-this is called the thing's nature. When the thing's nature is cultivated, it reverts to *teh*. When *teh* is complete, it is identified with the origin of things. From identification comes passivity (emptiness), and from passivity comes greatness....then all things are merged in continuous formlessness, seemingly devoid of all consciousness. This is called the Mystic Virtue which is identification with the Grand Harmony.

17. RULERS

Of the best rulers

The people (only) know[13] that they exist;
The next best they love and praise;
The next they fear;
And the next they revile.

When they do not command the people's faith,
Some will lose faith in them,
And then they resort to oaths!
But (of the best) when their task is accomplished, their work done,
The people all remark, 'We have done it ourselves.'

13 Some texts read: 'The people do not know.'

In Chapters 17, 18 and 19 Lao tzu discusses the decline of Tao and the world chaos resulting from the development of civilisation. This gives, particularly in Chapters 18 and 19, an exceptional opportunity for Chuang tzu to register his protest against the teachings of the sages and, in particular, against the Confucian teachings of humanity, justice, rituals and music. The fundamental viewpoint is that when man's original nature was yet unspoiled, he was acting in accord with Tao, obeying his instincts entirely, and therefore he was unconsciously good. The decline of Tao came with the development of knowledge and the consciousness of virtues and vices taught by the philosophers and the promotions and punishments instituted by governments. With the teaching of conscious virtues came hypocrisy, and with hypocrisy came world chaos.

17.1. EMPEROR YAO'S TEACHER. Yeh-ch'ueh met Hsu-yu (his disciple who was the teacher of Emperor Yao) and said to him, 'Where are you going?'
'I'm running away from Emperor Yao.'
'What do you mean?'

'The Emperor is so anxious to practice kindness and humanity,' replied Hsu-yu, 'I am afraid he is going to be the laughing-stock of the future generations. Centuries from now, we are going to see cannibalism. For it is not difficult to get the people to live peacefully with one another. If you arc kind to them, they will be close to you, and if you rule for their benefit, then they come. When you encourage them, they all like to do good, and if you force what is hateful on them, then they disperse. Those who can forget about humanity and justice are few and those who exploit the virtues of humanity and justice are many. When (the doctrines of) humanity and justice prevail, hypocrisy follows. And then, we resort to devices to induce them to do good, and it becomes possible for one man to decide and impose on the world what it regards as desirable, which in effect is like (surveying a given situation with) on wink of the eye. Yao knows what good the wise man can do to the world, but he does not realise what harm he can do.(6:15)

In accordance with the theory of continuous decline of Tao along with the development of civilisation, Emperor Yao was pictured as better than his successor, Emperor Shun, and Emperor Shun was pictured as better than his successor, Yu, etc. Consequently, in Chuang tzu's work, Emperor Yao was sometimes pictured as marking the beginning of the decline, and sometimes as coming before the decline.

17.2. EMPEROR YAO'S REIGN. In the reign of Yao, Pocheng Tsekao served as a duke under him. Yao was succeeded by Shun, who was succeeded by Yu. Pocheng Tsekao then gave up his title and retired as a farmer. Emperor Yu went to see him and found him working in the field. He ran up to him and, stopping below, stood still and asked, 'You served as a duke in the reign of Yao. Yao handed his throne to Shun, and Shun handed his throne to me. Why do you give up your title now and prefer to work on the farm? Tell me the reason.'

'In Yao's reign,' replied Tsekao, 'the people did right without inducement or reward, and they avoided the path of evil without threat of punishment. Now you have started promotions and punishments and the people have lost their natural humanity. Henceforth, man's character declines and punishments are instituted. This is going to be the beginning of world chaos. Why don't you go away and leave me alone?'

He went on tilling the field, and ignored his guest.

17.3. HOW MAN'S CHARACTER DECLINED. The ancient men lived in a world of primitive simplicity and the world was simple with them. That was the time when the *yin* and the *yang* worked harmoniously, and the spirits of men and beast did not interfere with the life of the people, when the four seasons were in order and all creation was unharmed, and the people did not die young. Although men had knowledge, they did not know what to do with it. This was the time of complete unity, when nobody interfered and people lived according to their nature. Then man's character began to decline. Then Suijen and Fuhsi (the legendary rulers who discovered the use of fire and domesticated animals respectively) came to rule the world. and the world still lived in accord with nature but had lost its unity. Man's character declined again. When the Emperors Shennung and Huangti (who taught agriculture and the use of silk, etc., respectively) came to rule the world, the world was still at peace, but was already departing from nature. Man's character declined again. Then Emperors Yao and Shun came to rule the world and began the spread of culture. Then falseness arose and the original simplicity of man was lost. Man departed from Tao in order to do good and performed commendable acts to win praise. Man abandoned nature and attended to the development of his mind. Mind rubbed against mind and produced knowledge, but as knowledge was not adequate to bring peace to the world, they resorted to cultural refinement and learning and scholarship. Cultural refinement destroyed the inner character of man and scholarship and learning submerged man's mind. From that time on, the people were perplexed and confused and lost the way whereby they could recover their original nature and return to the original state.(4:10)

17.4. CONVERSATION BETWEEN LAO TZU AND YANGTSE ON THE BEST RULER.

'Suppose there is a man here,' asked Yang Tsechu (Yangtse) of Lao tzu, 'who is strong and determined, who has insight and understanding of things and events, and follows Tao diligently Shall such a one be comparable to a wise ruler?'

'In comparison to the Sage, such a man is like a good clerk or a technical expert, who knows how to worry and to bustle about,' said Lao tzu. 'The proverb says,"tigers and leopards are hunted for their skins, the ape is captured for his agility, and the hound is put under leash because of his ability to worry foxes." How can such a person be compared to a wise ruler?'

Yangtse knitted his brows and said, 'Can you enlighten me on the kind of government by the wise ruler?

'In the government by the best ruler,' said Lao tzu, 'its effect is over the entire nation, yet it appears not to stem from him. He changes and influences all things, and the people are not dependent on him. His influence is there, but you cannot put your finger on it, and everybody is pleased with himself. (The ruler) is one who stands on the fathomless and roams in the sphere of not-being.' (2:11)

18. THE DECLINE OF TAO

On the decline of the great Tao,
    The doctrines of 'humanity' and 'justice'[14] arose.
When knowledge and cleverness appeared,
    Great hypocrisy followed in its wake.

When the six relationships no longer lived at peace,
    There was (praise of) 'kind parents' and 'filial sons.'
When a country fell into chaos and misrule,
    There was (praise of) 'loyal ministers.'

19. REALISE THE SIMPLE SELF

Banish wisdom, discard knowledge,
    And the people shall profit a hundredfold;
Banish 'humanity,' discard 'justice,'
    And the people shall recover love of their kin;
Banish cunning, discard 'utility,'
    And the thieves and brigands shall disappear.
As these three touch the externals and are inadequate;
    The people have need of what they can depend upon:
    Reveal thy simple self,[15]

14 Essential Confucian doctrines, usually translated (badly) as 'benevolence' and 'righteousness'.
15 Su, the unadorned, uncultured, the innate quality, simple self; originally 'plain silk background' as opposed to superimposed coloured drawings; hence the expression 'reveal,' 'realise', su.

> Embrace thy original nature,
> Check thy selfishness,
> Curtail thy desires.[16]

16 The eight characters in these four lines sum up practical Taoist teachings.

18.1. ON THE DECLINE OF THE GREAT TAO, THE DOCTRINES OF 'HUMANITY' AND 'JUSTICE' AROSE. And then when Sages appeared, straining for humanity and limping with justice, doubt and confusion entered men's minds. They said they must make merry by means of music and enforce distinctions by means of ceremony, and the empire became divided against itself. Were the uncarved wood not cut up, who could make sacrificial vessels? Were white jade left uncut, who could make the regalia of courts? Were Tao and character not destroyed, what use would there be for humanity and justice? Were men's natural instincts not lost, what need would there be for music and ceremonies? Were the five colours not confused, who would need decorations? Were the five notes not confused, who would adopt the six pitch-pipes? Destruction of the natural integrity of things for the production of articles of various kinds-this is the fault of the artisan. Destruction of Tao and character in order to strive for humanity and justice this is the error of the Sages. (3:3) *See the fuller context in 28.1*

18.2. THE ORIGIN OF HYPOCRISY. Action is man's nature in motion. When man's actions are false, it is called the loss of Tao.
    As an agent of man, it is easy to be false, but not as an agent of God.

There was a man who lived near the gate of Yen. When his parents died, he was rewarded with an office because (in his great show of filial piety) he disfigured himself. Because of that, many people in their town tried to follow his example when their parents died and half of them perished. (7:8)

The following two selections contain Chuang tzu's angry protests against civilisation. In both cases he specifically quoted Lao tzu's words: 'Banish wisdom, discard knowledge.' Exaggerated as the protest against civilisation is, the selection in 19.2 nevertheless contains a profound psychological truth. In exchange for the material essentials of civilised life, man has lost certain essentials which are necessary for his peace of mind. 19.1 is an extract from Chuang tzu's extraordinary essay, 'Opening trunks,' whose theme is, 'When the Sages arose, gangsters appeared.' 19.2 is an extract from his essay 'On Tolerance.'

19.1. 'OPENING TRUNKS.' The precautions taken against thieves who open trunks, search bags, or ransack cabinets, consist in securing with cords and fastening with bolts and locks. This is what the world calls wit. But a big thief comes along and carries off the cabinet on his shoulders, with box and bag, and runs away with them. His only fear is that the cords and locks should not be strong enough! Therefore, does not what the world used to call wit simply amount to saving up for the strong thief? And I venture to state that nothing of that which the world calls wit is otherwise than saving up for big thieves; and nothing of that which the world calls sage wisdom is other than hoarding up for robber.

How can this be shown? In the State of Ch'i, the neighbouring towns overlooked one another and one could hear the barking of dogs and crowing of cocks in the neighbouring town. Fishermen cast their nets and ploughmen ploughed the land in a territory of over two thousand *li*. Within its four boundaries, was there a temple or shrine dedicated, a god worshiped, or a hamlet, county or a district governed, but in accordance with the rules laid down by the Sages? Yet one morning T'ien Ch'engtse slew the ruler of Ch'i, and stole his kingdom. And not his kingdom only, but the laws of the Sages as well; so that although T'ien Ch'engtse acquired the reputation of a thief, he lived as securely and comfortably as ever did either Yao or Shun. The small States did not venture to blame, nor the great States to punish him, and for twelve generations his descendants ruled over Ch'i.[17] Was this not stealing the State of Ch'i together with the laws of the Sages in order to preserve their thieves' lives? I venture to ask, was there ever anything of what the world esteems as great wit otherwise than saving up for big thieves, and was there ever anything of what the world calls age wisdom other than hoarding up for robbers?

How can this be shown? Of old, Lungfeng was beheaded, Pikan was disemboweled, Changhung was sliced to death, Tsehsu was thrown to the waves. All these four were learned ones, but they could not preserve themselves from death by punishment.

An apprentice to Robber Cheh asked him, saying, 'Is there then Tao (moral principles) among thieves?'

'Tell me if there is anything in which there is not Tao.' Cheh replied. 'There is the sage character of thieves by which booty is located, the courage to go in first, and the chivalry of coming out last. There is the wisdom of calculating success, and kindness in the equal division of the spoils. There has never yet been a great robber who was not possessed of these five qualities.' Its seen therefore that without the teachings of the Sages, good men could not keep their position, and without the teachings of the Sages, Robber Cheh could not accomplish his ends. Since good men are scarce and bad men are the majority, the good the Sages do to the world is little and the evil great. Therefore it has been said, 'If the lips are turned up, the teeth will be cold.It was the thinness of the wines of Lu which caused the siege of Hantan.'[18]

When the Sages arose, gangsters appeared. Overthrow the Sages and set the gangsters free, and then will the empire be in

---

[17] There is an anachronism here, for Chuang tzu lived to see only the ninth generation of T'iens At least the number 'twelve' must have been slipped in by a later scribe.This evidence is not sufficient to vitiate the whole chapter, as some 'textual critics' claim.

[18] Reference to a story. The States, Lu and Chao, both presented wine to the King of Ch'u. By the trickery of a servant, the Hasks were exchanged, and Chao was blamed for presenting bad wine, and its city Hantan was besieged.

---

order. When the stream ceases, the gully dries up, and when the hill is levelled the chasm is filled. When the Sages are dead, gangsters will not appear, but the empire will rest in peace. On the other hand, if the Sages do not diminish, neither will the gangsters drop off. Nor if you double the number of Sages wherewith to govern the empire will you do more than double the profits of Robber Cheh.

If pecks and bushels are used for measurement, the pecks and bushels themselves will also be stolen, along with the rice. If scales and steelyards are used for weighing, the scales and steelyards themselves will also be stolen, along with the goods. If tallies and signets are used for good faith, the tallies and signets will also be stolen. If humanity and justice are used for moral principles, humanity and justice will also be stolen.

How is this so? Steal a hook and you hang as a crook; steal a kingdom and you are made a duke. (The teachings of) humanity and justice remain in the duke's domain. Is it not true, then, that they are thieves of humanity and justice and of the wisdom of the Sages?

So it is that those who follow the way of brigandage are promoted into princes and dukes. Those who are bent on stealing humanity and justice together with the measures, scales,tallies and signets can be dissuaded by no rewards of official regalia and uniform, nor deterred by fear of sharp instruments of punishment. This doubling the profits of robbers like Cheh,making it impossible to stop them, is the fault of the Sages.

Therefore it has been said, 'Fishes must be left in the water;the sharp weapons of a state must be left where none can see them.' These Sages are the sharp weapons of the world; they must not be shown to the world.

Banish wisdom, discard knowledge, and gangsters will stop! Fling away jade and destroy pearls, and petty thieves will cease. Burn tallies and break signets, and the people will revert to their uncouth integrity. Split measures and smash scales, and the people will not fight over quantities. Trample down all the institutions of Sages, and the people will begin to be fit for discussing (Tao). Confuse the six pitch-pipes, confine flutes and string instruments to the flames, stuff up the ears of Blind Shih K'uang, and each man will keep his own sense of hearing. Put an end to decorations, confuse the five colours, glue up the eyes of Li Chu, and each man will keep his own sense of sight.Destroy arcs and lines, fling away squares and compasses, snap off the fingers of Ch'ui the Artisan, and each man will use his own natural skill. Wherefore the saying, 'Great skill appears like clumsiness.' Cut down the activities of T'seng and Shih,pinch the mouths of Yang Chu and Motse, discard humanity and justice, and the character of the people will arrive at Mystic Unity.

If each man keeps his own sense of sight, the world will escape being burned up. If each man keeps his own sense of hearing, the world will escape entanglements. If each man keeps his intelligence, the world will escape confusion. If each man keeps his own virtue, the world will avoid deviation from the true path. Tseng, Shih, Yang, Mo, Shih K'uang, Ch'ui, and Li Chu were all persons who developed their external character and involved the world in the present confusion so that the laws and statutes are of no avail.

19.2. 'BE CAREFUL NOT TO INTERFERE WITH THE NATURAL GOODNESS OF THE HEART OF MAN.' Ts'ui Chu asked Lao Tan, saying, 'If the empire is not to be governed, how are men's hearts to be kept good?'

'Be careful,' replied Lao Tan (Lao tzu), 'not to interfere with the natural goodness of the heart of man. Man's heart may be forced down or stirred up. In each case the issue is fatal. By gentleness, the hardest heart may be softened. But try to cut and polish it, and it will glow like fire or freeze like ice. In the twinkling of an eye it will pass beyond the limits of the Four Seas. In repose, it is profoundly still; in motion, it flies up to he sky. Like an unruly horse, it cannot be held in check. Such is the human heart.'

Of old, the Yellow Emperor first interfered with the natural goodness of the heart of man, by means of humanity an justice. In consequence, Yao and Shun wore the hair off their legs and the flesh off their arms in endeavoring to feed their people's bodies. They tortured the people's internal economy in order to conform to humanity and justice. They exhausted the people's energies to live in accordance with the laws and statutes. Even then they did not succeed. Thereupon, Yao (had to) confine Huantou on Mount Ts'ung, exile the chiefs of the Three Miaos and their people into the Three Weis, and banish the Minister of Works to. Yutu, which shows he had not succeeded. When it came to the times of the Three Kings,the empire was in a state of foment. Among the bad men were Chieh and Cheh; among the good were Tseng and Shih, and the Confucianists and the Motseanists arose. Then came confusion between joy and anger, fraud between the simple and the cunning, recrimination between the virtuous and the evil minded, slander between the honest and the liars, and the world order collapsed.

When the man's original character lost its unity, men's lives were frustrated. When there was a general rush for knowledge,the people's desires ever went beyond their possessions. The next thing was then to invent axes and saws, to kill by laws and statutes, to disfigure by chisels and awls. The empire seethed with discontent, the blame for which rests upon those who interfered with the natural goodness of the heart of man.

In consequence, virtuous men sought refuge in mountain caves, while rulers of great states sat trembling in their ancestral halls. Then, when dead men lay about pillowed on each other's corpses, when cangued prisoners jostled each other in crowds and condemned criminals were seen everywhere, then the Confucians and the Motseans bustled about and rolled up their sleeves in the midst of handcuffs and fetters! Alas, they know not shame, nor what it is to blush!

Until I can say that the wisdom of Sages is not a fastener of cangues, and that humanity and justice are not handcuffs and shackles, how should I know that T'seng and Shih were not the singing arrows (forerunners) of (the gangsters) Chieh and Cheh? Therefore it is said, 'Abandon wisdom and discard knowledge, and the empire will be at peace.'

20. THE WORLD AND I

Banish learning, and vexations end.
    Between 'Ah!' and 'Ough!'
    How much difference is there?
Between 'good' and 'evil'
    How much difference is there?
That which men fear
    Is indeed to be feared;
But, alas, distant yet is the dawn (of awakening)!
The people of the world are merry-making,
    As if partaking of the sacrificial feasts.
    As if mounting the terrace in spring;
I alone am mild, like one unemployed,
    Like a new-born babe that cannot yet smile,
    Unattached, like one without a home.
The people of the world have enough and to spare,
But I am like one left out,
    My heart must be that of a fool,
    Being muddled, nebulous!
The vulgar are knowing, luminous;
    I alone am dull, confused.
The vulgar are clever, self-assured;
    I alone, depressed.
Patient as the sea,
    Adrift, seemingly aimless.
The people of the world all have a purpose;
    I alone appear stubborn and uncouth.
I alone differ from the other people,
    And value drawing sustenance from the Mother.[19]

19 Imagery of the sucking child, symbolising drawing power from Mother Nature.

20.1. THE DEMEANOUR OF THE MAN OF CHARACTER. The man of character lives at home without exercising his mind and performs actions without worry. The notions of right and wrong and the praise and blame of others do not disturb him. When within the four seas all people can enjoy themselves, that is happiness for him; when all people are well provided, that is peace for him. Sorrowful in countenance, he looks like a baby who has lost his mother; appearing stupid, he goes about like one who has lost his way. He has plenty of money to spend, and does not know where it comes from. He drinks and eats just enough and does not know where the food comes from. This is the demeanour of the man of character.

20.2. THE COMMON HERD OF MEN. The hypocrites are those people who regard as good whatever the world acclaims as good, and regard as right whatever the world acclaims as right.

When you tell them that they are men of Tao, then their countenances change with satisfaction; when you call them hypocrites, then they look displeased. All their lives they call themselves 'men of Tao,' and all their lives they remain hypocrites. They know how to give a good speech and tell appropriate anecdotes in order to attract the crowd, but from the very beginning to the very end, they do not know what it is all about. They put on the proper garb and dress in the proper colours and put on a decorous appearance in order to make themselves popular, but refuse to admit that they are hypocrites. They mingle with the crowd, and declare themselves in agreement with what the public likes and dislikes, at the same time claiming that they are better than the common men. Such is the height of their folly! Those who realise their folly are not true fools, and those who are conscious of their confusion are not truly confused. The truly confused can never get out of their confusion, and the genuine fools never recover from their folly. When three people are walking together and one of them is confused (or mistaken), it is still possible to go in the right direction, because only one is confused. When two of them are confused, then they cannot get anywhere because the confused ones are in the majority. Now the whole world is in confusion and although I have my hopes, I cannot attain them. Is this not a sad state of things? The highest kind of music cannot be appreciated by the ears of the villagers. But if you sing (the popular ditties) 'Break the Willow Branch' or 'The Gay Coloured Flowers,' they all open their mouths and laugh. Therefore, the highest teachings are not accepted by the minds of the common men, and the words of wisdom are not popular, because they are overshadowed by conventional teachings. And so people argue about the differences between two pints and one quart and end in nowhere. Now the world is in such confusion. Although I have my hopes, how can they be attained? Knowing that they cannot be attained, and trying to force them on the world, only adds to the confusion. Therefore, I shall leave it alone and yet when I leave it alone, who will share this sorrow with me? When the wife of a leper gives birth to a child at midnight, he brings a light along to look at the child, worried in his mind lest the child should not look at himself.

21. MANIFESTATIONS OF TAO

The marks of great Character[20]
Follow alone from the Tao.
The thing that is called Tao
   Is elusive, evasive.
Evasive, elusive,
   Yet latent in it are forms.
Elusive, evasive,
   Yet latent in it are objects.
Dark and dim,
   Yet latent in it is the life-force.
The life-force being very true,
   Latent in it are evidences.
From the days of old till now
Its Named (manifested forms) have never ceased,
By which we may view the Father of All Things.
How do I know the shape of Father of All Things?
   Through These ![21]

[20] Teh as manifestation of Tao, or Tao embodied, the moral principle, tr. by Waley as 'power.'
[21] Manifested forms.

This chapter is related in subject-matter to Chapter 14.

21.1. THROUGH INACTION THE HEAVEN BECOMES CLEAR.

Through inaction, the heaven becomes clear. Through inaction, the earth remains at peace. From the combination of the two in inaction, all things of the creation are acted upon. Evasive, elusive, do they not come from a source? Elusive, evasive, does not (the Tao) have a form? All things multiply and grow from inaction. Therefore, it is said, 'The heaven and earth do nothing and everything is done.' How can man learn this example of inaction?

21.2. THE LIFE-FORCE OF PERFECT TAO. The life-force of perfect Tao is profoundly mysterious; its extent is lost in obscurity.

21.3. THE CHARACTER OF TAO. For Tao has its inner reality and its evidences. It is devoid of action and of form. It may be transmitted, but cannot be received. It may be obtained, but cannot be seen. It is based in itself, rooted in itself. Before heaven and earth were, Tao existed by itself from all time. It gave the spirits and rulers their spiritual powers, and gave Heaven and Earth their birth. To Tao, the zenith is not high, nor the nadir low. Existing before the heaven and earth, it is not regarded as long ago; being older than the primeval beginnings, it is not regarded as old. (2:6)

22. FUTILITY OF CONTENTION

To yield is to be preserved whole.
To be bent is to become straight.
To be hollow is to be filled.
To be tattered is to be renewed.
To be in wan is to possess.
To have plenty is to be confused.

Therefore the Sage embraces the One,
And becomes the model of the world.
He does not reveal himself,
   And is therefore luminous.
He does not justify himself
   And is therefore far-famed.
He does not boast of himself,
   And therefore people give him credit.
He does not pride himself,
   And is therefore the chief among men.

It is because he does not contend
That no one in the world can contend against him.

Is it not indeed true, as the ancients say,
   'To yield is to be preserved whole?'
Thus he is preserved and the world does him homage.

In Chapters 22 and 24, the reader begins to see some of Lao tzu's paradoxes, of which more are yet to come. Behind all these paradoxes is the philosophy of eternal cycles, of things reverting to their opposites, as seen in Ch. 25 and in Ch. 40.

Some of the immediate applications of these paradoxes are the utility of futility, preservation through yielding, and the virtues of non-contention. The ultimate object is the preserving of one's life and one's character. This preservation through yielding to others is mentioned in the Prolegomena of Chuang tzu as one of the characteristics of Lao tzu's teaching.

22.1. THE UTITY OF FUTLITY. The mountain trees invite their own cutting down; lamp oil invites its own burning up.Cinnamon bark can be eaten; therefore the tree is cut down.Lacquer can be used; therefore the tree is scraped. All men know the utility of useful things; but they do not know the utility of futility.

Chuang tzu has a whole chapter devoted to the use of deformities.In many cases, it is a romanticist device to use physical deformities in contrast to inner spiritual perfection.

22.2. HUNCHBACK SU. THE VIRTUE OF DEFORMITIES

There was a hunchback named Su. His jaws touched his navel. His shoulders were higher than his head. His neck bone stuck out towards the sky. His viscera were turned upside down. His buttocks were on the same level with his ribs. By tailoring, or washing, he was able to earn his living. By sifting rice from husks he could make enough to support a family of ten. When orders came down for a conscription, the hunchback walked about unconcerned among the crowd. And similarly, in government conscription for public works, his deformity saved him from being called. On the other hand, when it came to government donations of grain for the disabled, the hunchback received as much as three *chung*, and of firewood, ten faggots. And if physical deformity was thus enough to preserve his body until the end of his days, how much more should moral and mental deformity avail!

Hunchback-Deformed-No-Lips spoke with Duke Ling of Wei and the Duke took a fancy to him. As for the well-formed men, he thought their necks were too scraggy. Big-Jar-Goitre spoke with Duke Huan of Ch'i, and the Duke took a fancy to him. As for the well-formed men, he thought their necks were too scraggy.

Thus it is that when virtue excels, the outward form is forgotten. But mankind forgets not that which is to be forgotten, forgetting that which is not to be forgotten. This is forgetfulness indeed! And thus the Sage sets his spirit free, while knowledge is regarded as extraneous growths; agreements are for cementing relationships, goods are only for social dealings, and the handicrafts are only for serving commerce. For the Sage does not contrive, and therefore has no use for knowledge; he does not cut up the world, and therefore requires no cementing of relationships; he has no loss, and therefore has no need to acquire; he sells nothing, and therefore has no use for commerce. These four qualifications are bestowed upon him by God, that is to say, he is fed by God. And he who is thus fed by God has little need to be fed by man. He wears the human form without human passions. Because he wears the human form he associates with men. Because he has not human passions the questions of right and wrong do not touch him. Infinitesimal indeed is that which belongs to the human; infinitely great is that which is completed in God.

22.3. TWO USELESS TREES. A certain carpenter Shih was travelling to the Ch'i State. On reaching Shady Circle, he saw a sacred *li* tree in the temple to the God of Earth. It was so large that its shade could cover a herd of several thousand cattle. It was a hundred spans in girth, towering up eighty feet over the hilltop, before it branched out. A dozen boats could be cut out of it. Crowds stood gazing at it, but the carpenter took no notice, and went on his way without even casting a look behind. His apprentice, however, took a good look at it, and when he caught up with his master, said, 'Ever since I have handled an adze in your service, I have never seen such a splendid piece of timber. How was it that you, Master, did not care to stop and look at it?'

'Forget about it. It's not worth talking about,' replied his master. 'It's good for nothing. Made into a boat, it would sink; into a coffin, it would rot; into furniture, it would break easily; into a door, it would sweat; into a pillar, it would be worm eaten. It is wood of no quality, and of no use. That is why it has attained its present age.'

When the carpenter reached home, he dreamt that the spirit of the tree appeared to him in his sleep and spoke to him as follows: 'What is it you intend to compare me with? Is it with fine-grained wood? Look at the cherry apple, the pear, the orange, the pumelo, and other fruit-bearers. As soon as their fruit ripens they are stripped and treated with indignity. The great boughs are snapped off, the small ones scattered abroad. Thus do these trees by their own value injure their own lives. They cannot fulfil their allotted span of years, but perish prematurely because they destroy themselves for the (admiration of) the world. Thus it is with all things. Moreover, I tried for a long period to be useless. Many times I was in danger of being cut down, but at length I have succeeded, and so have become exceedingly useful to myself. Had I indeed been of use, I should not be able to grow to this height. Moreover, you and I are both created things. Have done then with this criticism of each other. Is a good-for-nothing fellow in imminent danger of death a fit person to talk of a good-for-nothing tree?'

When the carpenter Shih awaken and told his dream, his apprentice said, 'if the tree aimed at uselessness, how was it that it became a sacred tree?'

'Hush!' replied his master. 'Keep quiet. It merely took refuge in the temple to escape from the abuse of those who do not appreciate it. Had it not become sacred, how many would have wanted to cut it down! Moreover, the means it adopts for safety is different from that of others, and to criticise it by ordinary standards would be far wide of the mark.'

Tsech'i of Nan-po was travelling on the hill of Shang when he saw a large tree which astonished him very much. A thousand chariot teams of four horses could find shelter under its shade.

'What tree is this?' cried Tsech'i. 'Surely it must be unusually fine timber.' Then looking up, he saw that its branches were too crooked for rafters; and looking down he saw that the trunk's twisting loose grain made it valueless for coffins. He tasted a leaf, but it took the skin off his lips; and its odour was so strong that it would make a man intoxicated for three days together.

'Ah!' said Tsech'i, 'this tree is really good for nothing, and that is how it has attained this size. A spiritual man might well follow its example of uselessness.

In the State of Sung there is a land belonging to the Chings, where thrive the catalpa, the cedar, and the mulberry. Such as are of one span or so in girth are cut down for monkey cages. Those of two or three spans are cut down for the beams of fine houses. Those of seven or eight spans are cut down for the solid (unjointed) sides of rich men's coffins. Thus they do not fulfil their allotted span of years, but perish young beneath the axe. Such is the misfortune which overtakes worth.

For the sacrifices to the River God, neither bulls with white foreheads, nor pigs with high snouts, nor men suffering from piles can be used. This is known to all the soothsayers, for these are regarded as *inauspicious*. The divine man, however, would regard them as extremely auspicious (to themselves).

22.4. THE ACCEPTANCE OF CONVENTIONS. To exalt the ancients and deprecate the moderns, that is the fashion for all scholars. For if one compares the modern world with the ancient world of Hsiwei, who would not be moved? But only the perfect man can go about in the modern world without attracting attention to himself. He accepts men's ways without loss of his self.

23. IDENTIFICATION WITH TAO

Nature says few words:
Hence it is that a squall lasts not a whole morning;
A rainstorm continues not a whole day.
Where do they come from?
From Nature.
Even Nature does not last long (in its utterances),
   How much less should human beings?[22]

Therefore it is that:
He who follows the Tao is identified with the Tao.
He who follows Character (*Teh*) is identified with Character.

He who abandons (Tao) is identified with abandonment (of Tao).
He who is identified with Tao-
   Tao is also glad to welcome him.
He who is identified with Character-
   Character is also glad to welcome him.
He who is identified with abandonment-
   Abandonment is also glad to welcome him.
He who has not enough faith
   Will not be able to command faith from others.

22 The meaning of this paragraph could be better understood in conjunction with the first two lines of the next chapter: 'He who stands on tiptoe does not stand firm; he who strains his stride does not walk well.'

24. THE DREGS AND TUMOURS OF VIRTUE

He who stands on tiptoe does not stand (firm);
He who strains his strides does not walk (well);
He who reveals himself is not luminous;
He who justifies himself is not far-famed;
He who boasts of himself is not given credit;
He who prides himself is not chief among men.
   These in the eyes of Tao
   Are called 'the dregs and tumours of Virtue.'
      Which are things of disgust.
Therefore the man of Tao spurns them.

23.1. DESCRIPTION OF A STORM. MUSIC OF THE EARTH.
   'The breath of the universe,' continued Tsech'i, 'is called wind. At times, it is inactive. But when active, all crevices resound to its blast. Have you never listened to its deafening roar?

'Caves and dells of hill and forest, hollows in huge trees of many a span in girth--some are like nostrils, and some like mouths, and others like ears, beam-sockets, goblets, mortars,or like pools and puddles. And the wind goes rushing through them, like swirling torrents or singing arrows, bellowing,sousing, trilling, wailing, roaring, purling, whistling in front and echoing behind, now soft with the cool blow, now shrill with the whirlwind, until the tempest is past and silence reigns supreme. Have you never witnessed how the trees and objects shake and quake, and twist and twirl?'

The thought in Chs. 22, 23, 24 is continuous, a warning against pride and ostentation.

24.1. ADVICE AGAINST OSTENTATION. The man who tries to show off his wealth is merely a merchant. People see him walking with big strides and call him a leader of the community.

Of the five vices, the vice of the mind is the worst. What is the vice of the mind? The vice of the mind is self-satisfaction.

24.2. TWO BARMAIDS. Yangtse went to Sung and stopped at an inn. There were two maid-servants, one of them very pretty, and the other very ugly. The ugly one occupied a higher position, while the pretty one did the chores. When Yangtse asked for the reason, the innkeeper's boy replied, 'The pretty one is conscious of her prettiness and therefore we don't think her pretty. The ugly one knows her ugliness and therefore we do not consider her ugly.'

24-3. 'HE WHO REVEALS HIMSELF IS NOT LUMINOUS.' THE DEFINITION OF 'GOOD.' Besides, were a man to apply himself to humanity and justice until he were the equal of Tseng or Shih, I would not call it good. Or to flavours, until he were the equal of Shu Erh (famous cook), I would not call it good. Or to sound, until he were the equal of Shih K'uang, I would not call it good. Or to colours, until he were the equal of Li Chu, I would not call it good. What I call good is not what is meant by humanity and justice, but taking good care of one's character. And what I call good is not the so-called humanity and justice, but fulfilling the instincts of life. What I call good at hearing is not hearing others but hearing oneself. What I call good at vision is not seeing others but seeing oneself. For a man who sees not himself but others, or takes possession not of himself but of others, possessing only what others possess and possessing not his own self, does what pleases others instead of pleasing his own nature. Now one who pleases others, instead of pleasing one's own nature, whether he be Robber Cheh or Po Yi, is just another one gone astray.

Conscious of my own deficiencies in regard to Tao, I do not venture to practice the principles of humanity and justice on the one hand, nor to lead the life of extravagance on the other. (3:2)

24.4. 'HE WHO BOASTS OF HIMSELF IS NOT GIVEN CREDIT'.

Confucius was in hiding in the plains between Ch'en and Tsai, and for seven days he (and his disciples) did not eat a hot meal. Taikung Jen went to see him during his trouble and said, 'You almost lost your life.'

'Yes.' relied Confucius.

'Do you hate to die?' asked Taikung Jen.

'Indeed,' replied Confucius.

'I'll teach you how to escape death,' said Jen. 'There is a raven in the eastern sea which is called Yitai ('dullhead'). This dullhead cannot fly very high and seems very stupid. It hops only a short distance and nestles close with others of its kind. In going forward, it dare not lead, and in going back, it dare not lag behind. At the time of feeding, it takes what is left over by the other birds. Therefore, the ranks of this bird are never depleted and nobody can do them any harm. A tree with a straight trunk is the first to be chopped down. A well with sweet water is the first to be drawn dry. Now you go about displaying your knowledge to frighten the ignorant people. You cultivate your virtue to show others at a disadvantage. Irradiating brilliance around you, you seem to go about carrying the sun and the moon in your hand. That is why you have got into trouble. I heard from the great master (Lao tzu): "He who boasts of himself is not given credit. The man who claims distinguished service falls and the man who achieves fame will be defamed." Who can abandon distinction for service and reputation and return to the common level of men? Tao pervades everywhere, and yet does not show itself. *Teh* (Tao manifest) influences everything and yet does not make its name known. Live sincerely and plainly like the others and suffer yourself sometimes to be called a fool. Avoid being conspicuous and keep away from a position of power. Do not live for service and fame. Thus you will not criticise others and others will not criticise you. The perfect man has no (thought of) reputation.'(5:9)

For another anecdote about the ostentation of Confucius, see 29.2.

25. THE FOUR ETERNAL MODELS

Before the Heaven and Earth existed
There was something nebulous:
   silent, isolated,
   standing alone, changing not,
   Eternally revolving without fail,

    Worthy to be the Mother of All Things.
I do not know its name
    And address it as Tao.
If forced to give it a name, I shall call it 'Great.'
Being great implies reaching out in space,
Reaching out in space implies far-reaching,
Far-reaching implies reversion to the original point.

Therefore: Tao is Great,
            The Heaven is great,
            The Earth is great,
            The King is also great,[23]
These are the Great Four in the universe,
And the King is one of them.
Man models himself after the Earth;
The Earth models itself after Heaven;
The Heaven models itself after Tao;
Tao models itself after Nature.[24]

23 *An ancient text reads 'man' in place of 'King.'*
24 *Tse-jan, lit. 'Self-so', 'self formed', 'that which is so by itself.'*

In this chapter, the working of the eternal principle of Tao and the silent revolutions of the heavenly bodies are seen as a model worthy of the imitation by man. It restates the argument that Tao should not be named, and if it is given a name, it is purely an exigency of human speech. It also states the principle of reversion of all things to their origin, a principle which makes creation and destruction different aspects of the same process.

25.1. THE MYSTERY OF THE UNIVERSE. Is the sky revolving around? Is the earth remaining still? Are the sun and the moon competing for their places? Who manages them? Who holds them in control? Who has nothing to do and is making these things move? Is it perhaps that there is a mechanism so that the heavenly bodies cannot help themselves? Is it perhaps that they continue to revolve and cannot stop themselves? Clouds become rain, and rain becomes clouds. Who makes them rise and come down? Who has nothing to do and is urging them to do so for his own pleasure? The wind rises from the north; it blows east and west, and there is a steady blow in the stratosphere. Who is sucking and blowing it alternately? Who has nothing to do and is shaking it about like this? (4.4)

Chuang tzu does not answer the questions directly, but in the following paragraph speaks of these operations of nature in a description of what he calls 'the heavenly Music' which ends with a quotation from an old sacred song of Yu-yen (Shen-nung). 'You listen and cannot hear its voice, you look and cannot see its form. It fills the whole universe and encompasses the six points of space. You want to listen to it, and yet there is no point of contact.'
See also the selection 6.1, 'The Silent, Beautiful Universe.'
'The heaven cannot help being high, the earth cannot help being wide. The sun and the moon cannot help going round, and all things of the creation cannot help but live and grow. Perhaps this is Tao.' See the context in 4.1.
'Existing before the heaven and earth, it is not regarded as long ago; being older than the primeval beginnings, it is not regarded as old.' See selection 21.2.

25.2. TAO IS NAMED 'GREAT' THE ETERNAL CYCLES.
'Can you then just call it Tao?' asked Little Knowledge.

'No,' replied Taikung Tiao. 'We speak of "The myriad things" of the creation, although we know that there are more than a myriad of them. Because the number is so great, we just call it "myriad." The heaven and earth are the great in form. The yin and yang are the great in force. Tao is great in both. We merely give it the name "Great" because of its greatness. But with a given name, it should not be compared with the names for other things. One cannot go on and argue that Tao is something by that name, as we say that dogs and horses are animals by those names. For that would be far off the mark.'

'Within the four points of the compass and above and below, how do the myriad things take their rise?' asked Little Knowledge.

'The yin and the yang principles act on one another, affect one another and keep one another in place. The four seasons follow one another in succession, inter-related in their coming and going. Hence arise likes and dislikes, and choices and preferences. The male and the female mate and the race is continued. Peace and chaos follow one another; fortune breeds misfortune and vice versa. The slow and the quick rub against each other and things are formed and disperse. These are some of the things that we can say about material things and some of the subtle principles that we can put down. All order is born of a principle, and all rise and decay are inter-related. When something reaches a limit, then it reverses its direction; when the end is reached, the beginning begins. This is all that is evidenced by the material world, all that we know and all that we can say. And after all, our knowledge does not extend beyond the material universe. He who observes the working of Tao does not try to follow a thing to its very end, nor trace it to its very source. There all discussion ends.' (7:4)

25.3. COMPLETE, ENTIRE AND ALL. The three, Complete, Entire and All differ in name, but are the same in reality. They all indicate the One. Once they roamed about together in the Palace of Nowhere. Did they get together to discuss things and never come to an end? Did they go about doing nothing together, and remain mellow and quiet, and indifferent and free? Did they get along well and spend their idle hours together?Free and unfettered is my mind, it reaches out and does not know where it reaches; it returns and does not know where it stops. My mind goes back and forth and does not know where it all ends. It loiters in the sphere of the Great Void, where the great Sage enters and does not know where it leads to. To realise that matter is matter is to reach the infinite with matter.Where matter is finite, it is the limitations of finite matter. The limit of the limitless is the limitlessness of the limited. To take the phenomena of rise and fall, growth and decay, it does not regard rise and fall as rise and fall, and it does not regard growth and decay as growth and decay. It does not regard beginning and end as beginning and end. It does not regard formation and dispersion as formation and dispersion. (6:3)

BOOK FOUR

THE SOURCE OF POWER

26. HEAVINESS AND LIGHTNESS

The Solid[1] is the root of the light;
The Quiescent is the master of the Hasty.

Therefore the Sage travels all day
   Yet never leaves his provision-cart[2].

In the midst of honour and glory,
    He lives leisurely, undisturbed.
How can the ruler of a great country
Make light of his body in the empire?³
In light frivolity, the Centre is lost;
In hasty action, self-mastery is lost.

1 Literally 'heavy,' with the Earth as model. In Chinese, 'heaviness' or 'thickness' of character, meaning 'honesty', 'generosity,' is associated with the idea of stable luck and endurance, whereas 'thinness' or 'lightness' of character, meaning 'frivolity' or 'sharpness', is associated with lack of sable luck.
2 A pun on the phrase, containing the word 'heavy.'
3 By rushing about.

26.1. NO HEED TO WORLDLY AFFAIRS. Chu Ch'iao addressed Ch'ang Wutse as follows: 'I heard Confucius say the true Sage pays no heed to worldly affairs. He neither seeks gain nor avoids injury. He asks nothing at the hands of man and does not adhere to rigid rules of conduct. Sometimes he says something without speaking and sometimes he speaks without saying anything. And so he roams beyond the limits of this mundane world. "These," commented Confucius, "are futile fantasies "But to me they are the embodiment of the most wonderful Tao' (1:9)

26.2. ON LETTING ONE'S SELF RUN AWAY WITH DESIRES OF THE BODY. The clever man is unhappy when he is not thinking of new ideas. The eloquent man is unhappy when he is not leading a discussion. The able man is not happy when he is not dealing with difficulties. They all bury themselves in the material things. The saviour of his country wants to make his country strong. The middle-class scholar wants to obtain official honour. The brave fighter wants to show off his prowess in an emergency. The brave man wants to volunteer himself in trouble. The soldier loves fighting. The retired scholar loves fame. The lawyer studies political science. The student of ceremonies attends to his appearance. The man of humanity and justice gives his time to social intercourse. The farmer is not happy when he is not tilling the field; the merchant is not happy when he is not making transactions in the market. The common man busies himself when he has something to do in the spare hours of the morning and evening, and the artisan feels good when he is working with his tools. When wealth is not hoarded, then the greedy rich is depressed; when he does not reach a position of power, then the self-important man is disappointed. These students of human affairs watch with happiness the changes of circumstances and the arrival of opportunity, and whenever they *can do something*, have a chance to do something, they cannot keep still. And so all these people follow their routine year in, year out, submerged in their own affairs, and cannot get out. They let their bodily desires run away with them and get tangled up in the thousand and one affairs until they die. Alas! (6:12)

'Calm represents the nature of water at its best,' see 8.1.

27. ON STEALING THE LIGHT
Good runner leaves no track.
A good speech leaves no flaws for attack.
A good reckoner makes use of no counters.
A Well-shut door makes use of no bolts,

And yet cannot be opened.
A well-tied knot makes use of no rope,
    And yet cannot be untied.
Therefore the Sage is good at helping men;
    For that reason there is no rejected (useless) person.
He is good at saving things;
    For that reason there is nothing rejected.[4]
    -This is called stealing[5] the Light.

Therefore the good man is the Teacher of the bad.
And the bad man is the lesson[6] of the good.

He who neither values his teacher
    Nor loves the lesson
Is one gone far astray,
    Though he be learned.
    -Such is the subtle secret.

4 *The Sage uses each according to his talent.*
5 *Hsi, to enter or secure by devious means such as invasion, attack at night, penetration, etc. The idea is cunningly to make use of knowledge of Nature's law to obtain the best results.*
6 *Tse, Raw-material, resources, help, something to draw upon for profit, such as a lesson.*

Without indulging in metaphysical terminology, Lao tzu is just as mystical as Chuang tzu. 'A good runner leaves no track,' etc., refers to the principle of reaching harmony and order without relying upon external devices and solutions. The futility of such devices is well shown in Chuang tzu's discussion of the futility of treaties for the purpose of keeping peace, see 19.I, or the futility of a disarmament conference where mutual suspicion exists, see 31.1. If peace, order, and the pursuit of happiness are invisible things, obviously they cannot be really obtained by visible means.

27.1. THE SAGE REJECTS NO PERSON. There was a man of the Lu State who had been mutilated, by the name of No-toes Shushan. He came walking on his heels to see Confucius; but Confucius said, 'You were careless, and so brought this misfortune upon yourself. What is the use of coming to me now?' 'It was because I was inexperienced and careless with my body that I injured my feet,' replied No-toes. 'Now I have come with something more precious than feet, and it is this that I am seeking to preserve. There is no man, but Heaven shelters him; and there is no man, but the Earth supports him. I thought that you, Master, would be like Heaven and Earth. I little expected to hear these words from you.'

'Pardon my stupidity,' said Confucius. 'Why not come in?I shall discuss with you what I have learned.' But No-toes left.

When No-toes had left, Confucius said to his disciples, 'Take a good lesson. No-toes is one-legged, yet he is seeking to learn in order to make atonement for his previous misdeeds. How much more should those seek to learn who have no misdeeds for which to atone?'

No-toes went off to see Lao Tan (Lao tzu) and said, 'Is Confucius a Perfect One or is he not quite? How is it that he is so anxious to learn from you? He is seeking to earn a reputation by his abstruse and strange learning, which is regarded by the Perfect One as mere fetters.'

'Why do you not make him regard life and death, and possibility and impossibility as alternations of one and the same principle,' answered Lao Tan, 'and so release him from those fetters?'

'It is God who has thus punished him,'replied No-toes. How could he be released?' (2.2)

Shent'u Chia had only one leg. He studied under Pohun Wujen ('Muddle-Head No-Such-Person') together with Tsech'an[7] of the State of Cheng. The latter said to him,'When I leave first, do you remain behind. When you leave first, I will remain behind.'

Next day, when they were again sitting together on the same mat in the lecture-room, Tsech'an said, 'When I leave first, do you remain behind. Or if you leave first. I will remain behind. I am now about to go. Will you remain or not? I notice you show no respect to a high personage. Perhaps you think yourself my equal?'

'In the house of the Master, replied Shent'u Chia, 'there is already a high personage (the Master). Perhaps you think you are the high personage and should take precedence over the rest. I have heard that if a mirror is perfectly bright, dust will not collect on it; if it does, the mirror is no longer bright. He who associates for long with the wise should be without fault.   Now you have been seeking the greater things at the feet of our Master, yet you can say things like that. Don't you think you are making a mistake?'

> 7 A well-known historical person, a model minister referred to in the Analects.

'You are already mutilated,' retorted Tsech'an, 'yet you are still seeking to compete in virtue with Yao. To look at you, I should have thought you had enough to do to reflect on you past misdeeds!'

'Those who cover up their sins,' said Shent'u Chia 'so as not to lose their legs, are many in number. Those who forget to cover up their misdemeanours and so lose their legs (through punishment) are few. But only the virtuous man can recognize the inevitable and remain unmoved. People who walked in front of the bull's-eye when Hou Yi (the famous archer) was shooting would be hit. Some who were not hit were just lucky. There are many people with sound legs who laugh at me for not having them. This used to make me angry. But since I came to study under our Master, I have stopped worrying about it. Perhaps our Master has so far succeeded in purifying me with his goodness. At any rate, I have been with him nineteen years without being aware of my deformity. You and I are roaming in the realm of the spiritual, and yet you are judging me by the standards of the physical. Are you not committing a mistake?'

At this Tsech'an began to fidget and his countenance changed, and he bade Shent'u Chia to speak no more. (2:1)

28. KEEPING TO THE FEMALE

He who is aware of the Male
But keeps to the Female
   Becomes the ravine[8] of the world.
Being the ravine of the world,
   He has the original character[9] which is not cut up,
   And returns again to the (innocence of the) babe.

He who is conscious of the white (bright)
But keeps to the black (dark)
   Becomes the model for the world.
Being the model for the world,
   He has the eternal power which never errs.
   And returns again to the Primordial Nothingness.

He who is familiar with honour and glory
But keeps to obscurity
   Becomes the valley of the world.
Being the valley of the world,
   He has an eternal power which always suffices,
And returns again to the natural integrity of uncarved wood.
Break up this uncarved wood
   And it is shaped into vessel
In the hands of the Sage,
   They become the officials and magistrates.
   Therefore the great ruler does not cut up.

8 See Ch. 6. *The valley, or ravine, is symbol of the Female Principle, the receptive,the passive.*
9 *Teh.*

   Read as a whole, the emphasis in Book Four is on guarding the source of power, which is the unspoiled nature of man. The theme is especially clear in this chapter, and in Chs. 32 and 37.

In the interesting essay entitled 'Horse's Hoofs,' Chuang tzu discusses the idea of preserving man's original nature by comparing the harm done to that nature by the Confucianists and the harm done to a horse by a famous horse trainer. Lao tzu's imagery of preserving the 'natural integrity' of the 'uncarved wood' and not 'cutting it up' is given in identical phraseology and more forcefully developed.

The Prolegomena by Chuang tzu mentions 'being aware of male, but keeping to the female', 'being the ravine of the world,' etc., as among the basic teachings of Lao tzu.

28.1. THE HORSE-TRAINER POLO. Horses have hoofs to carry them over frost and snow, and hair to protect them from wind and cold. They feed on grass and drink water, and fling up their tails and gallop. Such is the real nature of horses. They have no use for ceremonial halls and big dwellings

One day Polo (famous horse-trainer)[10] appeared, saying, 'I am good at managing horses.' So he burned their hair and clipped them, and pared their hoofs and branded them. He put halters around their necks and shackles around their legs and numbered them according to their stables. The result was that two or three in every ten died. Then he kept them hungry and thirsty, trotting them and galloping them, and taught them to run in formation, with the misery of the tasselled bridle in front and the fear of the knotted whip behind, until more than half of them died.

The potter says, 'I am good at managing clay. If I want it round, I use compasses; if rectangular, a square.' The carpenter says, "I am good at managing wood. If I want it curved, I use an arc; if straight, a line.' But on what grounds can we think that the nature of clay and wood desires this application of compasses and square, and arc and line? Nevertheless, every

10 Sun Yang, 658-619 B.C.

age extols Polo for his skill in training horses, and potters and carpenters for their skill with clay and wood. Those who manage (govern) the affairs of the empire make the same mistake.

I think one who knows how to govern the empire should not do so. For the people have certain natural instincts--to weave and clothe themselves, to till the fields and feed themselves. This is their common character, in which all share. Such instincts may be called 'Heaven-born.' So in the days of perfect nature, men were quiet in their movements and serene in their looks. At that time, there were no paths over mountains, no boats or bridges over waters. All things were produced, each in its natural district. Birds and beasts multiplied; trees and shrubs thrived. Thus it was that birds and beasts could be led by the hand, and one could climb up and peep into the magpie's nest. For in the days of perfect nature, man lived together with birds and beasts, and there was no distinction of kind. Who could know of the distinctions between gentlemen and common people? Being all equally without knowledge, their character could not go astray. Being all equally without desires, they were in a state of natural integrity. In this state of natural integrity, the people did not lose their (original) nature.

And then when Sages appeared, straining for humanity and limping with justice, doubts and confusion entered men's minds. They said they must make merry by means of music and enforce distinctions by means of ceremony, and the empire became divided against itself. Were the uncarved wood not cut up, who could make sacrificial vessels? Were Tao and character not destroyed, what use would there be for humanity and justice? Were man's natural instincts not lost, what need would there be for music and ceremonies? Were the five notes not confused, who would adopt the six pitch-pipes? Destruction of the natural integrity of things for the production of articles of various kinds- this is the fault of the artisan. Destruction of Tao and character in order to strive for humanity and justice--this is the error of the Sages. (3:3)

'To know it is to cut it up,' *see 16.3.*

28.2. ON RETURNING TO NATURE. 'What do you mean by nature or the natural? And what do you mean by man, or the artificial?' asked the River Spirit.

And the Spirit of the North Sea replied, 'When a cow or a horse walks about with his four legs (in freedom), we call it nature. To put a halter around the horse's head and put a ring through the cow's nose, that we call the artificial. Therefore its said, do not let the artificial submerge the natural. Do not for material purposes destroy your life. Do not sacrifice your character for fame. Guard carefully your nature and do not let it go astray. This is called returning to one's nature.' (4:13)

29. WARNING AGAINST INTERFERENCE

There are those who will conquer the world
And make of it (what they conceive or desire).
    I see that they will not succeed.
(For) the world is God's own Vessel
It cannot be made (by human interference).
    He who makes it spoils it.
    He who holds it loses it.
For: Some things go forward,
    Some things follow behind;
    Some blow hot,
    And some blow cold.[11]
    Some are strong,
    And some are weak;
    Some may break,
    And some may fall.
Hence the Sage eschews excess,
              eschews extravagance,
              eschews pride.

[11] Literally, 'blow out,' ' blow in.' follow Waley's rendering, which conveys the meaning perfectly.

In Chapters 29, 30 and 31, Lao tzu's thoughts are directed to war which arises because man forgets the advice against interference and strife and contention. In these chapters, Lao tzu say some of the best things that have ever been said about war.

29.1. TO HAVE TERRITORY IS TO HAVE SOMETHING GREAT.

For to have a territory is to have something great. He who has something great must not regard the material things as material things. Only by not regarding material things as material things can one be the lord of things. The principle of looking at material things as not real things is not confined to mere government of the empire. Such a one may wander at will between the six limits of space or travel over the Nine Continents, unhampered and free. This is to be the Unique One. The Unique One is the highest among men. (3:8)

In various anecdotes, Confucius constantly comes in for castigation for his desire to show off his knowledge. Two have been told in 24.3.
Here is another one.

29.2. ANECDOTE ABOUT CONFUCIUS.

A disciple of Laolaitse[12] was gathering firewood one day when he met Confucius.

He returned and told his master, 'There is a man out there who is tall on top and squatty below. His back stoops and his ears are set backwards. He has a look in his eyes as if he was going to manage the whole universe. I don't know whose son he is.'

'That is Ch'iu (Confucius),' said Lao tzu. 'Ask him to come.'

When Confucius arrived, Lao tzu said, 'Ch'iu, forget your pride and your look of wisdom. Then you may look like a gentle man.'(7:6)

[12] *A few scholars essay the opinion that Laolaise was identical with Lao tzu, but there is no conclusive evidence to prove it. The advice given by Laolaitse to Confucius it his passage, however, is similar to the advice given by Lao tzu to him as recorded by Szema Ch'ien in Hsiki.*

30. WARNING AGAINST THE USE OF FORCE

He who by Tao purposes to help the ruler of men
Will oppose all conquest by force of arms.[13]
For such things are wont to rebound.

Where armies are, thorns and brambles grow.
The raising of a great host
Is followed by a year of dearth.[14]

Therefore a good general effects his purpose and stops.
    He dares not rely upon the strength of arms;
Effects his purpose and does not glory in it;
Effects his purpose and does not boast of it;
Effects his purpose and does not take pride in it;
    Effects his purpose as a regrettable necessity;
    Effects his purpose but does not love violence.
(For) things age after reaching their prime.
That (violence) would be against the Tao.
And he who is against the Tao perishes young

13 The Chinese character for 'military' is composed of two parts: 'stop' and 'arms.' Chinese pacifists interpret this as meaning disapproval of arms ('stop armament'), whereas it may just as well mean to 'stop' the enemy 'by force.' Etymologically, however, the word for 'stop' is a picture of a footprint, so the whole is a picture of a 'spear'. over 'footprints.'
14 These six lines are by Waley, for they cannot be improved upon.

31. WEAPONS OF EVIL

Of all things, soldiers[15] are instruments of evil,
    Hated by men.
Therefore the religious man (possessed of Tao) avoids them.
The gentleman favours the left in civilian life,
But on military occasions favours the right.[16]

Soldiers are weapons of evil.
    They are not the weapons of the gentleman.
When the use of soldiers cannot be helped,
    The best policy is calm restraint.

Even in victory, there is no beauty,[17]
And who calls it beautiful

Is one who delights in slaughter.
He who delights in slaughter
   Will not succeed in his ambition to rule the world.

[The things of good omen favour the left.
The things of ill omen favour the right.
The lieutenant-general stands on the left,
The general stands on the right.
That is to say, it is celebrated as a Funeral Rite.]
The slaying of multitudes should be mourned with sorrow.
A victory should be celebrated with the Funeral Rite.[18]

>15 Another reading, 'fine weapons.' Ping can mean both 'soldiers' and 'weapons.'
>16 These are ceremonial arrangements. The left is a symbol of good omen, the creative; the right is a symbol of bad omen, the destructive.
>17 Another equally good reading: 'no boasting,' 'and who boasts of victory.'
>18 One of the five Cardinal Rites of Chou-Ii. The last five lines but two read like a commentary, interpolated in the text by mistake. The evidence is conclusive: (I) The terms 'lieutenant general' and 'general' are the only ones in the whole text that are anachronisms, for these terms did not exist till Han times. (2) The commentary by Wang Pi is missing in this chapter, so it must have slipped into the text by a copyist's mistake. See also Ch. 69. Cf. Mencius, 'The best fighter should receive the supreme punishment'; again, 'Only he who does not love slaughter can unify the empire.'

30.1. THE DANGER OF RELYING ON AN ARMY. The Sage is never sure of what others regard as sure; hence, he does not rely on an army. The common men are sure of what one cannot be sure about; hence, a big army. When an army is there, it is against human nature not to try to get what one wants. And when one relies on the army, one perishes. (8:13)

31.1. ON THE EMPTINESS OF VICTORY.
   'I have long wanted to meet you,' said Duke Wu of Wei (known for his war exploits, speaking to Hsu Wukuei). 'I love my people and follow righteousness. I am thinking of disarmament. What do you think?'

'You cannot do it,' replied Hsu Wukuei. 'To love the people is the beginning of hurting them. To plan disarmament in the cause of righteousness is the beginning of rearmament. If you start from there, you will never accomplish anything. The love of a good name is an instrument of an evil. Although Your Highness wishes to follow the doctrine of humanity and justice, I am afraid you are going to end in hypocrisy. The material leads to the material; pride comes with accomplishment, and war comes with the change of circumstances. Do not parade your soldiers before the Towers of Lich'iao; do not display your infantry and cavalry in the palace of Chut'an. Do not obtain things by immoral means. Do not gain your end by astuteness, by strategy, or by war. For to slaughter the people of another country, take their territory in order to increase one's private possessions and please oneself-what good will such a war do? In what does such a victory consist? You should leave it alone, and search within yourself, and let things fulfil their nature without your interference. Thus the people will already have escaped death. What need will there be for disarmament?'(6:11)

Chuang tzu's argument against disarmament may appear fallacious on the surface, but is fundamentally correct. When it becomes necessary to talk of disarmament, all plans of disarmament must fail, as man has learned today. His argument is essentially that of moral rearmament.
   In the followings selection, the dilemma of war or peace is presented even more forcefully. The situation of two thousand pears ago, when preparedness for war and unpreparedness for war seemed equally reckless, is reminiscent of today.

31.2. THE DILEMMA OF WAR AND PEACE.

Wei Yung (King Huei of Wei) signed a treaty with T'ien Houmou (King Wei of Ch'i, a powerful state) and T'ien broke it. Wei Yung was a angry and was going to send someone to assassinate him. His lion-head (a general's title) felt ashamed when he heard of it, and said to him, 'You are a ruler of a country with ten thousand chariots and you are thinking of revenge by assassination. If you will give me an army of two hundred thousand men, I am going to attack them. I shall capture his people as slaves and drive away his cattle and horses and make him burn with shame and chagrin. And then, we shall raze his city. When Chi(T'ien) flees his country, I shall smash his back and break his spine.'

Chitse felt ashamed when he heard of this and said, 'Somebody built a city wall of ten *jen* and then you want to tear it down. What a waste of human labour! Now there has been no war for seven years and this seems a good beginning for building up a strong country. Yen (the officer) is a reckless fellow. Don't listen to him.'

Huatse felt ashamed when he heard of this and said, 'The man who talks about invading Chi'i is a reckless person. The man who talks about not invading Ch' is also a reckless person. The man who calls them both reckless persons is also a reckless person himself.'

'Then what am I going to do?' said the King.

'Just seek the Tao,' replied Huatse.

Hueitse (Chuang tzu's friend, a great sophist) heard about this and went to see Tai Chinjen (and told him how to speak to the King).

(Following Hueitse's advice) Tai Chinjen said to the King, 'Have you ever heard of a thing called the snail?'

'Yes.'

'There is a kingdom at the tip of the left feeler of the snail. Its people are called the Ch'us. And there is a kingdom at the tip of the right feeler of the snail, and its people are called the Mans. The Ch'us and the Mans have constant wars with one another, fighting about their territories. When a battle takes place, the dead lie about the field in tens of thousands. The defeated army runs for fifteen days before it returns to its own territory.'

'Indeed.' said the King. "Are you telling me a tall tale?'

'It isn't a tall tale at all. Let me ask you, do you think there is a limit to space in the universe?'

'No limit,' replied the King.

'If you could let your mind roam about in infinity, and arrive in the Country of Understanding, would not your country seem to exist and yet not to exist?'

'It seems so,' replied the King.

'In the centre of the Country of Understanding, there is your country, Wei, and in the country of Wei there is the city of Liang, and in the centre of the city of Liang, there is the king. Do you think there is any difference between that king and the king of the Mans?'

'No difference,' replied the King.

The interviewer withdrew and the King felt lost. (7:2)

32. TAO IS LIKE THE SEA

Tao is absolute and has no name.
Though the uncarved wood is small,
    It cannot be employed (used as vessel) by anyone.
If kings and barons can keep (this unspoiled nature),
    The whole world shall yield them lordship of their own accord.

The Heaven and Earth join,
    And the sweet rain falls,
Beyond the command of men,
    Yet evenly upon all.

Then human civilisation arose and there were names.[19]
Since there were names,
    It were well one knew where to stop.
He who knows where to stop
    May be exempt from danger.
Tao in the world

May be compared to rivers that run into the sea.[20]

This chapter repeats the theme of guarding man's unspoiled nature, stated in Chapter 28, and should be read in conjunction with it and with Chapter 37. As stated here, the ruler or the Sage who keeps his original nature unspoiled acquires some kind of a mystic power or virtue which is felt as an all-pervading influence in his country.

19 Names imply differentiation of things and loss of original state of Tao.
20 Really to be compared to the sea, or to the rivers seeking repose in the sea.

From the following selection, one can easily see the difference between Tao and Teh, usually translated as 'character.' Tao is the unembodied principle, while Teh is the principle embodied. Consequently, Tao is unknowable, while Teh is knowable.

32.1. SEEK REPOSE IN WHAT THE HUMAN MIND CANNOT KNOW. Character always leads up to the unity represented by Tao, and knowledge must seek repose in what the human mind cannot know. That represents the limit of knowledge. What is unified in Tao becomes differentiated in Teh. What the human consciousness cannot know, it is impossible for words to express. It is fatal for the Confucians and the Motseans to argue with one another in a bid for fame and reputation. Therefore, the great sea does not object to flowing eastwards: that is why it is great. The Sage encompasses the entire universe and his influence is felt throughout the world, and yet we do not know his family name. Therefore, in his lifetime, he has no rank, and after his death, he receives no posthumous title. He accumulates nothing and does not make a name for himself. Such is what we call a great man. A dog is not considered good because of his barking, and a man is not considered clever because of his ability to talk. How much more is it true of one who is great? One who considers himself great cannot be considered great. How much more is this true of the man of Teh (or character)? To be great is to be complete in itself. What is more self-sufficient than the universe, but does it ever seek for any thing in order to achieve all-sufficiency? One who knows the truth about all-sufficiency seeks nothing, loses nothing, and rejects nothing. He does not allow his own nature to be affected by material things. He seeks it within himself and finds infinity there; he follows the ancients but he is not servile to them. Such is the substance of the great man. (6:14)

Note that the line, 'The great sea does not object to flowing eastwards,' or downwards, serves to clarify the meaning of the last two lines of this chapter. Because the great sea always flows downwards, it is therefore like the Tao. See Ch. 66.

One of the most important ideas of Chuang tzu is the limitation of knowledge, or his agnosticism or scepticism regarding knowledge itself.Chuang tzu says over and over again that there is the world of knowable and the world of unknowable, that the world of knowable represents finite knowledge, but the important truths of God and of the universe belong in the world of unknowable, and that, therefore,the latter stands on a much higher plane than the former.

32.2. 'KNOWING WHERE TO STOP' CHUANGU TZU'S SAYINGS ON THE UNKNOWABLE.

Human life is limited, but knowledge is limitless. To drive the limited in pursuit of the limitless is fatal; and to presume that one really knows is fatal indeed!

One who knows how to stop at where he cannot know has reached the limit of knowledge. (6:7)

What man knows is very little. Although that knowledge is little, man must rather depend on what he does not know before he can know the meaning of God. (6:16)

What we can know compared with what we cannot know is but like a squint (compared with the fill view of a situation)(6:9)

33. KNOWING ONESELF

He who knows others is learned;
   He who knows himself is wise.
He who conquers others has power of muscles;
   He who conquers himself is strong.
He who is contented is rich.
   He who is determined has strength of will.
He who does not lose his centre endures,
He who dies yet (his power) remains has long life.

In this chapter, Lao tzu gives a number of aphorisms on knowledge and learning, strength, wealth, and his definition of long life. It is clear that the line 'He who dies yet his power remains has long life,' comes very near to Lao tzu's definition of immortality; here Lao tzu gives a slight twist to the Chinese word shou, or 'long life,' which in the Chinese mind is considered one of the greatest blessings on earth. Like all great poet-philosopher, Chuang tzu felt even more keenly than Lao tzu the shortness and pathos of man's transient life and he was keenly affected by the subject of death. Certainly some of Chuang tzu's best writings touched upon the subject of life and death, about which Lao tzu had comparatively little to say.

'He who knows others is learned; he who knows himself is wise.' This line is already clarified in Chapter 24.

33.1. ON WEALTH AND POVERTY. Yuan Hsien was living in Lu in a little shack. Its roof was covered with green grass, and the reed screen for its door was tattered. A mulberry trunk served for the door hinge and a broken jar served for his window. The house had two rooms and the window was stuffed with rags. The roof leaked and the floor was damp. But Yuan Hsien sat properly in it and was playing on a string instrument. One day Tsekung (a successful diplomat and a disciple of Confucius) came to see him, riding on a big horse and wearing a navy blue gown with a white coat on top. His big carriage could not go through the narrow alley. Yian Hsien came out to meet him with a briar stick in his hand and wearing a hemp cap and a pair of shoes without heels.

'Alack-a-day! What ails you?' said Tsekung.

'Nothing ails me,' replied Yian Hsien. 'I have heard that to have no money is called poverty, but to know the truth and be not able to follow it is called a disease. I am poor but not sick.'

Tsekung felt a little embarrassed and loitered for a moment and Yuan Hsien laughed. 'You know that there are certain things that I cannot do,' he said. 'These are: to go about the world and do things to win the public's praise; to go about socially and form a circle of friends; to study for others' sake and to teach for one's own sake; to do evil under the cloak of humanity and justice; and to enjoy the luxury of a beautiful carriage. These things I cannot do.' (8:3)

'The contented man does not land himself in involvements on account of money.' (8:3)

Emperor Yao went to visit Hua and the officer of Hua said to him, 'Welcome, Sage! May I offer you some toasts? I drink to your long life.'

'Please don't,' said Emperor Yao.

'Then I drink to your wealth,'

'Please don't.' replied Yao

'Then may I wish you many male children?'

Emperor Yao again declined.

'Why, these three things, a long life, wealth and having many male children, are desired by everybody,' said the officer. 'Why are you an exception?'

'To have many male children is to have many worries,' replied Yao. 'To have wealth is to be occupied with many affairs. To have a long life is to live to see many humiliations. All these three things are not conducive to the development of one's character. That is why I have declined.'

'I thought you were a sage,' said the officer, 'but now I know you are only a gentleman. Since God has created the people, He must have something for each one to do. If you have many sons, let each find something to do. Why should you let that worry you? If you have a lot of money, share it with others. Then what business will you have to attend to? A sage lives like a partridge (without a constant abode) and he eats like a young bird (contented with what the mother bird gives him). He goes about like a bird (without definite destination) and does not declare himself. When the world is in order, he prospers along with all things, and when the world is in chaos, he cultivates his character and leads a leisurely life. After a thousand years, when he is bored with this earthly life, he becomes a fairy. Riding upon white clouds, he arrives at God's abode. The three kinds of trouble cannot reach him and he is preserved from harm. How can he suffer from humiliation?'

Saying this, the officer left. Yao followed him and said, 'May I talk to you?'

'Get away,' said the officer. (3:11)

It may be noted that following the Taoist notion of taking things as they come, a follower should not reject even wealth. In Chuang tzu's works, Lao tzu is once pictured as living in plenty with a full granary.(4:3)

In the following, I have gathered together a few of the many sayings of Chuang tzu about death. What he says about life and death will be found in Ch. 50. Chuang tzu's remarks about the skull remind one of the sayings of Hamlet about Yorick.

33.2. THE SKULL. Chuang tzu went to Ch'u and saw an empty skull with a sharp contour. He struck it with a horse-whip and asked, 'How did you come to this? Did you live an extravagant life and abuse your constitution? Were you a condemned criminal and killed by the executioner? Did you do something wrong which shamed your parents and your wife and children (and commit suicide)? Or did you die of hunger and starvation? Or did you live to an old age and die a natural death?'

After saying this, he took the skull and used it as a pillow and lay down to sleep. At midnight, the skull appeared to him in a dream, and said to him, 'You talked like a sophist. What you mentioned are the troubles of mortal life. When one dies, one does not have such troubles. Do you want to hear about life after death?'

'Yes,' replied Chuang tzu

'In death,' said the skull, 'there are no kings and no subject and no change of seasons. One is completely free, regarding heaven and earth as spring and autumn. Such happiness exceeds even that of a king.'

Chuang tzu would not believe him and said, 'If I asked the controller of life to restore your body, give you bones and flesh and skin, return you to your parents and family and let all your neighbourhood know about it, would you like it?'

The skull knitted its brows and deepened its eyes and said,'How can I exchange the happiness of a king for the troubles of the mortal world?' (5:2)

33.3. CHUANG TZU'S WIFE DIED. Chuang tzu's wife died and Hueitse went to offer his condolence. The visitor found him squatting on the ground and singing, beating on a basin to keep time.

'Someone has lived with you and raised children for you and now her old body dies. Is it not enough that you should not weep, but that you should be singing to the music of a basin? Isn't it too much?'

'No,' replied Chuang tzu. 'When she died, how could I help but feel very sorry? But I began to think and I realized that originally she had no life, and not only no life, she had no form, and not only no form, she had no spirit (*yin* and *yang*). She was a part of a mass of formlessness. Then she changed and received spirit, the spirit changed, and she was given form, form changed and she was given life, and now she changes once more and goes to her death. She merely goes through a process resembling the rotation of spring, summer, autumn and winter. There she lies now peacefully in a big house. If I should break down and cry aloud, I would behave like one who does not understand destiny. Therefore, I stopped. (5:1)

33.4. CHUANG TZU WAS ABOUT TO DIE. Chuang tzu was about to die, and his disciples wanted to give him a sumptuous funeral.

'I regard the heaven and earth as my coffin and outer coffin.the sun and the moon as a pair of jade gifts and the constellations as my burial jewels. And the whole creation shall come to my funeral. Will it not be a grand funeral? What more should I want?'

'We are afraid that vulture crows will come and eat our master,' said the disciples.

'Above the ground, I shall be eaten by the vultures, and underground, I shall be eaten by the ants. Why rob the one to give it to the other? Why are you so partial (to the ants)?' Chuang tzu replied. (8:15)

33.5. LAO TZU DIED. When Lao tzu died, Ch'in Yi went to the funeral. He uttered three yells and departed.

A disciple asked him, saying, 'Were you not our Master's friend?'

'I was,' replied Ch'in Yi.

'And if so, do you consider that a sufficient expression of grief at his death?' added the disciple.

'I do,' said Ch'in Yi. 'I had thought he was a (mortal) man, but now I know that he was not. When I went in to mourn, I found old persons weeping as if for their children, young ones wailing as if for their mothers. In such a situation, certain words naturally escape our mouths and tears naturally escape our eyes. But to do so (To cry thus at one's death) is to evade the natural principles (of life and death) and increase human attachments, forgetting the source from which we receive this life. The ancients called this "evading the retribution of Heaven." The Master came, because it was his time to be born; he went, because it was his time to go away. Those who accept the natural course and sequence of things and live in obedience to it are beyond joy and sorrow. The ancients spoke of this as the emancipation from bondage.' (1:11)

33.6. THE CONVERSATION OF FOUR FRIENDS ON LIFE AND DEATH.

Four men: Tsesze, Tseyu, Tseli and Tselai, were conversing together, saying, 'Whoever can make Not-being the head, Life the backbone, and Death the tail, and whoever realize that death and life and being and non-being are of one body, that man shall be admitted to friendship with us.' The four looked at each other and smiled, and completely understanding one another, became friends accordingly.

By and by, Tseyu fell ill, and Tsesze went to see him. 'Verily the Creator is great!' said the sick man. 'See how He has doubled me up.' His back was so hunched that his viscera were on top, his chin was hidden in his navel, and his shoulders were higher than his head. His neck bone pointed up towards the sky. The whole economy of his organism was deranged, but his mind was calm as ever. He dragged himself to a well, and said, 'Alas, that God should have doubled me up like this!'

'Do you dislike it?' asked Tsesze.

'No. why should I?' replied Tseyu. 'if my left arm should become a cock, I should be able to herald the dawn with it. If my right arm should become a sling, I should be able to shoot down a bird to broil with it. If my buttocks should become wheels, and my spirit become a horse, I should be able to ride in it-what need would I have of a chariot? I came to life because it was my time, and I am now parting with it in the natural course of things. Content with the coming of things in their time and living in accord with Tao, joy and sorrow touch me not. This is, according to the ancients, to be freed from bondage.[21] Those who cannot be freed from bondage are so because they are bound by the trammels of material existence.But man has ever given away before God; why, then, should I dislike it?'

By sod by, Tselai fell ill and lay gasping for breath, while his family stood weeping around. Tseli went to see him, and cried to the wife and children: 'Go away! You are impeding is dissolution.' Then, leaning against the door, he said, 'Verily,God is great! I wonder what He will make of you now, and whither He will send you. Do you think he will make you into a rat's liver or into an insect leg?'

'A son,' answered Tselai, 'must go whither soever his parents bid him, East, West, North or South. *Yin* and *yang* are no other than a man's parents. If *yin* and *yang* bid me die quickly,and I demur, then the fault is mine, not theirs. The Great (universe) gives me this form, this toil in manhood, this repose in old age, this rest in death. Surely that which is such a kind arbiter of my life is the best arbiter of my death.

'Suppose that the boiling metal in a smelting-pot were to bubble up and say, "Make of me a Moyeh!"[22] The master caster would reject that metal as uncanny. And if simply because I am cast into a human form, I were to say, "Only a man! only a man!" the Creator, too, would reject me as uncanny. If I regard the universe as the smelting-pot, and the Creator as the Master Caster, how should I worry wherever I am sent?' Then he sank into a peaceful sleep and waked up very much alive. (2:7)

21 Compare the identical lines in 33.5.
22 a famous sword.

33-7. THE CONVERSATION OF THREE FRIENDS ON LIFE AND DEATH

Tsesang Hu, Mengtse Fan and Tsech'in Chang, were conversing together, saying, 'Who can live together as if they did not live together? Who can help each other as if they did not help each other? Who can mount to heaven, and roaming through the clouds, leap about in the Ultimate Infinite, oblivious of existence, for ever and ever without end?' The three looked at each other and smiled with a perfect understanding and became friends accordingly.

Shortly afterwards, Tsesang Hu died, whereupon Confucius sent Tsekung to attend the mourning. But Tsekung found that one of his friends was arranging cocoon sheets and the other was playing string instruments and (both were) singing together as follows:

'Oh! come back to us, Sang Hu,
Oh! come back to us, Sang Hu,
Thou hast already returned to thy true state,
While we still remain here as men! Oh!'

Tsekung hurried in and said, 'How can you sing in the presence of a corpse? Is this good manners?'

The two men looked at each other and laughed, saying, 'What should this man know about the meaning of good manners, indeed?' Tsekung went back and told Confucius, asking him, 'What manner of men are these? Their object is to cultivate nothingness and let their minds wander beyond their corporeal frames. They can sit near a corpse and sing, unmoved. There is no name for such persons. What manner of men are they?'

'These men,' replied Confucius, 'roam about beyond the material things; I move about within them. Consequently, our paths do not meet, and I was stupid to have sent you to mourn. They consider themselves companions of the Creator, and wander about within the One Spirit of the universe. They look upon life as a huge goitre or excrescence, and upon death as the breaking of a tumour. How could such people be concerned about the coming of life and death or their sequence?

They borrow their forms from the different elements, and take temporary abode in the common forms, unconscious of their internal organs and oblivious of their senses of hearing and vision. They go through life backwards and forwards as in a circle without beginning or end, strolling forgetfully beyond the dust and dirt of mortality, and playing about with the affairs of inaction. How should such men bustle about the conventionalities of this world for people to look at?'

'But if such is the case,' said Tsekung, 'which world (the corporeal or the spiritual) would you deal with?'

'I am one condemned by God,' replied Confucius. 'Nevertheless, I will share with you (what I know).'

'May I ask what is your method?' asked Tsekung.

'Fishes live their full life in water. Men live their full life in Tao,' replied Confucius. 'Those that live their full life in water thrive in ponds. Those that live their full life in Tao achieve realisation of their nature in inaction. Hence the saying "Fish lose themselves (are happy) in water; man loses himself (is happy) in Tao."'

'May I ask,' said Tsekung, 'about (those) strange people?'

'(Those) strange people,' replied Confucius, 'are strange in the eyes of man, but normal in the eyes of God. Hence the saying that the meanest person in heaven would be the best on earth; and the best on earth, the meanest in heaven.' (2:8)

34. THE GREAT TAO FLOWS EVERYWHERE
The Great Tao flows everywhere,

(Like a food) it may go left or right.
The myriad things derive their life from it,
    And it does not deny them.
When its work is accomplished,
    It does not take possession.
It clothes and feeds the myriad things,
    Yet does not claim them as its own.
Often (regarded) without mind or passion,[23]
    It may be considered small.
Being the home[24] of all things, yet claiming not,
    It may be considered great.
Because to the end it does not claim greatness,
    Its greatness is achieved.

23 Compare Ch.1.
24 Literally 'All things return, or belong, to it.'

34.1. THE IMMANENCE OF TAO.

'Where is this so-called Tao?' asked Tungkuotse of Chuang tzu.
'Tao is everywhere,' replied Chuang tzu.
'But you must specify.'
'It is in the ants,' was the reply.
'Why, is it so low?'
'It is in the tare-seeds,' said Chuang tzu again.
'It is getting lower still,' exclaimed Tungkuotse.
'Tao is in the jars and bricks.'
'It is getting worse and worse!'
'It is in the excrements.' said Chuang tzu.

    Tungkuotse did not speak any more, and Chuang tzu said 'What you asked just now is a question which is a difficult one for me to answer and substantiate with examples. When Corporal Huo went to the head of the market to buy pigs, he looked for the pig's hoofs (as the best place to judge a pig). You should not have asked me to specify, for thus you cannot get away from the material. Great truths are (elusive) like this, and so are great teachings.' (6:3)

34.2. TAO IS EVERYWHERE. At its greatest, Tao is infinite; at its smallest, there is nothing so small but Tao is in it. That is how the myriad things come. It is so big that it encompasses everything. Deep like the sea, it cannot be fathomed. (4:4)

'The greatest reaches of space do not leave its confines, and the smallest down of a bird in autumn awaits its power to assume form.' *See selection 6.1.*

35. THE PEACE OF TAO

Hold the Great Symbol[25]
   And all the world follows,
   Follows without meeting harm,
   (And lives in) health, peace, commonwealth.

Offer good things to eat
And the wayfarer stays.
   But Tao is mild to the taste.
   Looked at, it cannot be seen;
   Listened to, it cannot be heard;
   Applied, its supply never fails.

[25] *The symbol of Nature, Heaven or Earth. This chapter consists of rhymed three-word lines.*

Liehtse, or the author of the works which go by that name, develops especially that part of the Taoist teachings which emphasize the control of mind over matter. In Chuang tzu's works, he appears as a fairy riding upon the winds. Kuanyin was the officer of the pass who persuaded Lao tzu to write the Book of Tao. *See the Prolegomena.*

35.1. PEACE THROUGH HOLDING THE TAO.
'The perfect man goes about unknown in the world, and meets no obstacles,' spoke Liehtse to Kuanyin. 'He steps on fire without feeling its heat, and walks upon great height without fear. How is he able to do that?'

'That comes of perfect concentration of the spirit,' replied Kuanyin. 'It belongs entirely in a different order from human cunning and physical courage. Let me tell you. All those which have sound, colour and appearance are material things. One material thing cannot be very far from another material thing,and one cannot reach from it to the non-sensuous world(However), things are created out of the formless and return to the changeless. Who holds it (Tao) and pursues its study readily cannot be hindered by the material things.. .. A drunken man falls from a carriage, and though he may be hurt,it is not fatal. His bones are the same as those of other men, but he does not suffer the same injuries, because his spirit is whole. He is neither aware of riding in a carriage, nor of falling from it. Life and death, and worries and fears, do not trouble his breast; therefore he meets obstacles without fear. If even he who achieves wholeness of spirit through wine can do this,how much easier it is for one who has achieved that wholeness of spirit through Nature!

'The Sage takes shelter in Nature; therefore he is above all harm. The avenger does not wreak his vengeance on the sword and shield (of his enemy); even the most spiteful man does not bear a grudge against the flying tile (which happens to hit him).Therefore the world lives at peace; when it follows the Tao,the ravages of war are unknown and there are no punishments by death. Do not develop the nature which is of man, but develop the nature which is of God. From the development of that which is of God, character follows; from the development of that which is of man, harm follows. If the people keep to that which is of God persistently and do not neglect that which is of man, they may come near to realising their purity.(5:4)

The result of mingling action and inaction, of living both above the world and in it by necessity, is a state of mind called 'mildness' or 'mellowness' which is the chief virtue of a Taoist. Mildness, calm,quietude and inaction are used together and almost interchangeably,as will be seen in selection 37.1. As the Tao is mild, so is the Taoist.

35.2. TEMPER KNOWLEDGE WITH MILDNESS. The ancients who practised the Tao, strengthened their knowledge by mildness. To strengthen one's knowledge by mildness means that one realises one has to live, but does not depend on the cunning of the mind. When knowledge and (the love of) mildness strengthen each other, then the peaceable temperament is brought out from man's nature. (4:9)

35.3. 'APPLIED, ITS SUPPLY NEVER FAILS.'
'To be poured into without becoming full, and pour out without becoming empty, without knowing how this comes about-this is the art of preserving the Light.' *See selection 5.2.*

36. THE RHYTHM OF LIFE

He who is to be made to dwindle (in power)
    Must first be caused to expand.
He who is to be weakened
    Must first be made strong,
He who is to be laid low
    Must first be exalted to power.
He who is to be taken away from
    Must first be given,
    -This is the Subtle Light.

Gentleness overcomes strength:
    Fish should be left in the deep pool,
    And sharp weapons of the state should be left
        Where none can see them.

In this chapter we see a full expression of the practical consequences of the doctrine of universal reversion. In Chuang tzu's beautiful essay 'Autumn Floods,' after a long development of the relativity of standards and distinctions, he comes to the following conclusion.

36.1. THE DOCTRINE OF REVERSION.

'Shut up, Uncle River. What do you know about the distinctions of the higher-class and lower-class houses and between the big and the small families?' concluded the Spirit of the North Sea.

'Then what should I do, and what should I not do? What should I accept, and what should I reject? What am I going to do?' asked the River Spirit.

'From the point of view of Tao,' says the Spirit of the North Sea, 'What is higher class, and what is lower class? For this is the doctrine of reversion. Do not clutter up your mind with hard and fast notions, for this would be running opposite to Tao. What is much and what is little? Be grateful (to Heaven) for what you have. Do not follow stubbornly one course of movement, for this would be to deviate from Tao. Be strict with yourself, impartial like the ruler of a country, and at ease; like the sacrifice at the God of Earth, where prayers are offered for the common good. Flow everywhere, in the vast and limitless expanse, abolishing all boundaries. Love all creation equally.' (4:13)

'To take the phenomena of rise and fall, growth and decay, it does not regard rise and fall as rise and fall, and it does not regard growth and decay as growth and decay. It does not regard beginning and end as beginning and end. It does not regard formation and dispersion as formation and dispersion.' See selection 25.3.

'These are all levelled together by Tao. Division is the same as creation, and creation is the same as destruction. There is no such thing as creation and destruction, for these conditions are again levelled together into One.' See 2.1.

36.2. TO BE UNITED IS TO BE PARTED. 'In the nature of things and in the known tradition of human affairs, it is different. To be united is to be parted. To be completed is to be destroyed. To be sharp-edged is to be blunted. To be in an elevated position is to be criticised. To do is to impair. To be eminent is to be plotted against. To be stupid is to be taken advantage of. Alas, is there anything in this human world that we can regard as sure? Remember, my disciples, take refuge only in the village of Tao and character,' says Chuang tzu. (5:8)

36.3. SIGNS OF FAILURE AND SUCCESS. There are eight signs of failure, and three signs of success. The body contains six internal organs. Beauty, a long beard, tallness, size, strength, grace, courage, daring-those who excel others in these eight are doomed to failure. Conservatism, compliance and caution, feeling oneself not the equal of others-these three are the signs of success. (8:15)

37. WORLD PEACE

The Tao never does,
    Yet through it everything is done,
If princes and dukes can keep the Tao,
    The world will of its own accord be reformed.
When reformed and rising to action,
    Let it be restrained by the Nameless pristine simplicity.
The Nameless pristine simplicity
    Is stripped of desire (for contention).
By stripping of desire quiescence is achieved,
And the world arrives at peace of its own accord.

From the preceding chapters, there is a kind of running argument that quiescence and inaction represent the state of unspoiled nature, the source of all power. It has also become clear that as we live in the human world, total abstention from activities is impossible, and so one comes to the resultant attitude of a mild passivity and indulgent quietness as the wisest mode of life. In the following selection, we have probably the most complete description of the doctrine of inaction, based on the imitation of nature and the silent workings of the universe, and recommending calm passivity and a mild and mellow attitude as the wise man's way of life.

37.1. THE DOCTRINE OF INACTION AND QUIETUDE. The heaven revolves and does not accumulate; hence the things of the creation are formed. The ruler of a state lets things run their course and does not accumulate; therefore the world follows and obeys him. The sage's influence circulates everywhere and does not accumulate; therefore the world pays him homage.

To understand the way of nature and of the sage and to see the changes of the elements in time and space and apply them to the way of a ruler is to realise that each thing runs its own course and there is a state of quietude amidst all the activities. The sage is calm not because he says to himself, 'It is good to be calm,' and therefore chooses to be so. He is naturally calm because nothing in the world can disturb his mind. When water is at repose, it is so clear that it can reflect a man's beard; it maintains absolute level and is used by the carpenter for establishing the level. If water is clear when it is at rest, how much more so is the human spirit? When the mind of the sages is calm, it becomes the mirror of the universe, reflecting all within it.

Passivity, calm, mellowness, detachment and inaction characterise the things of the universe at peace and represent the height of development of Tao and character. Therefore the ruler and the sage take their rest therein. To take rest is to be passive; passivity means having reserve power, and having reserve power implies order. Passivity means calm and when calm reverts to action, every action is right. Calm means inaction, and when the principle of inaction prevails, each man does his duty. Inaction means being at peace with oneself, and when one is at peace with oneself, sorrows and fears cannot disturb him and he enjoys long life.

Passivity, calm, mellowness, detachment and inaction represent the root of all things. By understanding them Yao became an emperor, and Shun a good minister. In the position of power, these become the attributes of the emperor, the son of heaven; in the position of the common man, these become the attributes of the sage and philosopher-king. One retires with these virtues, and all the scholars at leisure in the hills and forests and rivers and seas admire him. One assumes office to put the world in order, and he accomplishes great results and the world become unified. He keeps quiet and becomes a sage, he acts and become a king. If he does nothing and guards carefully his original simplicity, no one in the entire world can compete with him in beauty of character. For such a one understands the character of the universe. This is called the great foundation and the great source of all being. That is to be in harmony with God. To bring the world into order, that is to achieve harmony with men. To be in harmony with men is the music of man, and to be in harmony with God is the music of God. Chuang tzu says, 'Ah! my Master, my Master! He trims down all created things, and does not account it justice. He causes all created things to thrive and does not account it kindness. Dating back further than the remotest antiquity, He does not account himself old.Covering heaven, supporting earth, and fashioning various forms of things, He does not account himself skilled.' This is called the music of heaven. Therefore, it is said, 'He who understands the music of heaven lives in accordance with nature in his life and takes part in the process of change of things in his death.' In repose, his character is in harmony with the *yin* principle; in activity, his movement is in harmony with the *yang* principle. Therefore he who understands the music of heaven is not blamed by heaven or criticised by men, or burdened with material affairs or punished by the ghosts. Therefore it is said, 'In action he is like heaven. In repose he is like the earth. Because his mind has found repose he becomes the king of the world. His departed ghost does not appear to disturb others, and his spirit does not know fatigue. Because his mind has found repose, therefore the creation pays homage to him.' That is to say, passivity and calm are principles that run through the heaven and earth and all creation. That is the music of heaven. The music of heaven is that by which the sage nourishes all living things. (4:1)

37.2. 'THE WORLD ARRIVES AT PEACE OF ITS OWN ACCORD'. THE IMITATION OF NATURE. Though heaven and earth are great, they act impartially on all things. Though the things of the creation are many, the principle of peace is the same. Though the people in a nation are many, their sovereign is the king. The king imitates Teh (the character of Tao) and lets things be completed according to nature. Therefore it is said. 'The kings of primitive times did nothing.' In that, they were only following the character of nature. By judging the names of titles and ranks in the light of Tao, the king's position becomes established. By judging the distinction of position in the light of Tao, the duties of the king and his ministers become clear. By judging ability in the light of Tao, the officials of the country carry out their duties. By judging everything in the light of Tao, all things respond to our needs. Therefore character is that which is related to heaven and earth, and Tao is that which pervades all creation.
....Therefore it is said, 'In ancient times, those who helped in sustaining the life of the people had no desires themselves and the world lived in plenty, did nothing, and all things were reformed, remained deep at rest and the people lived at peace.' (3:9)

38. DEGENERATION

The man of superior character is not (conscious of his)
   character,
   Hence he has character.
The man of inferior character (is intent on) not losing character,
   Hence he is devoid of character.
The man of superior character never acts,
   Nor ever (does so) with an ulterior motive.
The man of inferior character acts,
   And (does so) with an ulterior motive.

The man of superior kindness acts,
   But (does so) without an ulterior motive.
The man of superior justice acts,
   And (does so) with an ulterior motive.
(But when) the man of superior *li*[26] acts and finds no response,
   He rolls up his sleeves to force it on others.

Therefore:
After Tao is lost, then (arises the doctrine of) humanity,
After humanity is lost, then (arises the doctrine of) justice.
After justice is lost, then (arises the doctrine of) *li*.
Now *li* is the thinning out of loyalty and honesty of heart.
   And the beginning of chaos.
The prophets are the flowering of Tao
   And the origin of folly.

[26] Li, Confucian doctrine of social order and control, characterised by rituals; also courtesy, good manners.

Therefore the noble man dwells in the heavy (base),
   And not in the thinning (end).
He dwells in the fruit,
   And not in the flowering (expression).
Therefore he rejects the one and accepts the other.

This is one of the best-known chapters of Lao tzu and in many editions which divide the works into two books, it marks the beginning of the second book. This division, I find, is no accurate. I believe that all the important philosophical principles which form the basis of Lao tzu's philosophy are covered in the first forty chapters; after Chapter 40, the book deals with more practical questions like the conduct of life and the theory of government.

The subject of this chapter is the decline of Tao through the rise of the conscious teachings of philosophers, especially the basic Confucian teachings of 'humanity,' 'justice,' 'ceremonies' and 'music'. It should be read in conjunction with Chapters 18 and 19 where the selections from Chuang tzu voice his angry protest against Confucianism.

38.1. THE DECLINE OF TAO. Tao cannot be reached. Teh cannot be achieved. Humanity can be cultivated. Justice can be deficient and rituals are means of affectation. Therefore, it is said, 'After Tao is lost, then arises Teh; after Teh (or character) is lost, then arises the doctrine of humanity; after humanity is lost, then arises the doctrine of justice; after justice is lost, then arises the doctrine of rituals.' Rituals represent the decadent flowering of Tao and the beginning of world chaos. (6:1)

The above quotation is evidently from Lao tzu, because it is verbally identical with the text in this chapter, and it occurs together with several other quotations which can also be found in Lao tzu's book.

38.2. THE PROPER PLACB OF HUMAN INSTITUTIONS. The primary things should stand at the top and secondary things stand at the bottom. The essential principles should be with the sovereign;

the details with the ministers. The three armies and five kinds of military weapons are things that belong to the means of government. Promotions and punishments, inducements and rewards and the criminal code are the secondary things in a nation's culture. Rituals and laws, the distinctions of rank and statistics and the comparison of terminology are secondary things in the art of government. Bells and drums and feather decorations are the secondary things in music. Weeping and mourning and the wearing of hemp clothes and hemp hemming and the gradations in the length of mourning are secondary things in the expression of sorrow. These five kinds of secondary things require the employment of the mind and conscious planning before they can be carried out. The ancients had this body of the unessential knowledge, but they did not put it first. ... To talk about Tao without observing the sequence of importance is to miss Tao. To discuss Tao and miss it at the same time-of what use could be the discussion? Therefore, the ancients who understood the great Tao first tried to understand nature, and then to understand Tao and Teh. After they understood Tao and Teh, then they began to understand humanity and justice. After humanity and justice were understood, then they began to attend to differences of ranks an duties. After the differences in ranks and duties were established, then they tried to set the terminology in order. When the terminology was established, then they began to decide on appointments. After appointments were made, then they began to review the records of the personnel. After their records were reviewed, then they tried to decide right and wrong. After they decided right and wrong, then they considered the promotions and punishments. When the promotions and punishments were properly carried out, then the clever and the stupid ones, the high and the low, the good and the bad, all fell into their proper places, each employing his ability and acting according to his station. Thus those above may be served, those below may be properly fed, affairs may be attended to, the self may be cultivated, and there is no need to rely on cunning and strategy and all credit is given to God. This is the reign of peace, the height of the art of government. Therefore, an ancient book says, 'When there is form, there is a name.' The ancients had this science of forms and names, but they did not put it first. In speaking of the great principles (of government), according to the ancients, the science of terminology was the fifth step and promotions and punishments came in the ninth. To begin by talking about terminology (as the Confucians do) is to fail to appreciate the fundamentals. To begin by talking of promotions and punishments is to fail to recognise the foundation. This is to reverse entirely the sequence of Tao. Such (technicians of government) should serve others; how could they be the rulers? To begin by talking of terminology and promotions and punishments is to know the means of government without knowing the principles of government. They can be employed for the government, but cannot govern the world. These people are merely specialists. (4:2)

38.3. HOW CONFUCIAN DOCTRINES LEAD TO CHAOS.

Besides, love (over-refinement) of vision leads to debauchery in colour; love of hearing leads to debauchery in sound; love of humanity leads to confusion in character; love of justice leads to perversion of principles; love of ceremonies (*li*) leads to a common fashion for technical skill; love of music leads to common lewdness of thought; love of wisdom leads to a fashion for the arts; and love of knowledge leads to a fashion for criticism. If the people are allowed to fulfil peacefully the natural instincts of their lives, the above eight may or may not be; it matters not. But if the people are not allowed to fulfil peacefully the natural instincts of their lives, then these eight cause discontent and contention and strife, and throw the world into chaos.

Yet the world worships and cherishes them. Indeed, the mental chaos of the world is deep-seated. Is it merely a passing mistake that can be simply removed? Yet they observe facts before their discussion, bend down on their knees to practice them, and sing and beat the drum and dance to celebrate them. What can I do about it? (3:6)

For further opposition of Taoist and Confucian ideas, see the section, Imaginary Conversations of Lao tzu and Confucius.

Taoism lays great emphasis on unconscious goodness, goodness that is natural and without motivation. The moment goodness is motivated, it is regarded as a decline or deviation from Tao.

38.4. UNCONSCIOUS GOODNESS. To arrive there (in Tao) without realising why it is so is called Tao. (1:6)

There is no greater injury to one's character than practising virtue with motivation. (8:14)

Chuang tzu says, 'In archery, the man who hits the target without aiming first is the good archer.' (6:12)

A man feels a pleasurable sensation before he smiles, and smiles before he thinks how he ought to smile. (2:9)

39. UNITY THROUGH COMPLEMENTS

There were those in ancient times possessed of the One:
    Through possession of the One, the Heaven was clarified,
    Through possession of the One, the Earth was stabilised,
    Through possession of the One, the gods were spiritualised,
    Through possession of the One, the valleys were made full,
Through possession of the One, all things lived and grew,
Through possession of the One, the princes and dukes became the ennobled of the people.
-That was how each became so.

Without clarity, the Heavens would shake,
Without stability, the Earth would quake,
Without spiritual power, the gods would crumble,
Without being filled, the valleys would crack,
Without the life-giving power, all things would perish,
Without the ennobling power, the princes and dukes would stumble.
Therefore the nobility depend upon the common man for support,
And the exalted ones depend upon the lowly for their base.

That is why the princes and dukes call themselves 'the
   orphaned,' 'the lonely one,' 'the unworthy.'
Is it not true then that they depend upon the common man for
   support?
Truly, take down the parts of a chariot,
   And there is no chariot (left).[27]
Rather than jingle like the jade,
   Rumble like the rocks.

27 Another commonly accepted reading through word-substitution in the text: 'Truly, the highest prestige requires no praise.' Apart from the forced substitution of words, this reading makes no sense in the context.

39.1. THE POWER OF TAO. Hsi Wei obtained Tao, and so set the universe in order. Fu Hsi [28] obtained it, and was able to steal the secrets of eternal principles. The Great Dipper obtained it. and has never erred from its course. The sun and moon obtained it, and have never ceased to revolve. K'an P'i[29] obtained it, and made his abode in the K'unlun mountains.
P'ing I[30] obtained it, and rules over the streams. Chien Wu[31] obtained it, and dwells on Mount T'ai. The Yellow Emperor[32] obtained it, and soared upon the clouds to heaven. Chuan Hsu[33] obtained it, and dwells in the Dark Palace. Yu Ch'iang[34] obtained it, and established himself at the North Pole. The Western (Fairy) Queen Mother obtained it, and settled at Shao Kuang, since when and until when, no one knows. P'eng Tsu obtained it, and lived from the time of Shun until the time of the Five Princes. Fu Yueh obtained it, and as the Minister of Wu Ting[35] extended his rule to the whole empire. And now, charioted upon the Tungwei (one constellation) and drawn by the Chiwei (another constellation), he has taken his station among the stars of heaven. (2:6)

28 Mythical emperor (2852 B.C.) said to have discovered the principles of mutations of Yin and Yang.
29 With a man's head, but a beast's body.
30 A river spirit.
31 A mountain god.
32 A semi-mythical ruler, who ruled in 2698-2597 B.C

33 A semi-mythical ruler, who ruled in 2514-2437 B.C., shortly before Emperor Yao.
34 A water god with a human face and a bird's body.
35 A monarch of the Shang Dynasty, 1324-1206 B.C.

39.2. THE POWER BEHIND SPRING AND AUTUMN. 'My disciple, why are you so surprised?' said Kengsangch'u (a disciple of Lao tzu). 'Spring comes and all vegetation grows. Autumn arrives and the harvest is taken in. Now, do you suppose spring and autumn do these things without something behind them?' (6:5)

39.3. HOW A SAGE LIVES IN THE WORLD. Jan Hsiang held firm to the centre and took things as they came along. He was unaware of the beginning and the end and the past and the present. He followed the process of change in nature, but in keeping to the One, he knew that the One was eternal and changeless. He did not forget the unity of things for a moment. For one who tries to model himself after nature and fails, perishes with the common things and loses the power with which to meet the affairs of the day. For a sage is unconscious of nature and of man, of beginnings and of material things. He goes about in this world without falling back and in all that he does, he never fails. That is how he keeps close to the Tao. (7:1)

40. THE PRINCIPLE OF REVERSION

Reversion is the action of Tao.
    Gentleness is the function of Tao.
The things of this world come from Being,
    And Being (comes) from Non-being.

This chapter seems to be the summing up of Lao tzu's teachings in a nutshell. Most basic of all is the statement of the principle of reversion as the operation of Tao. This has been clarified already in selections 25.2, 25.3 and 36.1. See especially the selection 25.2, 'The eternal cycle,' and the statement, 'All inspiring, the cycle begins again when it ends.' (4.1)

40.1. REVERSION IS THE ACTION OF TAO. And all things being equal, how can one say which is long and which is short? Tao is without beginning, without end. The material things are born and die, and no credit is taken for their development. Emptiness and fullness alternate, and their relations are not fixed. Past years cannot be recalled; time cannot be arrested. The succession of growth and decay, of increase and diminution, goes in 'a cycle, each end becoming a new beginning. In this sense only may we discuss the ways of truth and the principles of the universe. The life of things passes by like a rushing, galloping horse, changing at every turn, at every hour. What should one do, or what should one not do? Let the (cycle of) changes go on by themselves! (4:13)

40.2. THE ORIGIN OF THINGS. EVOLUTION OF BEING FROM NOT BEING.

'Do you suppose,' asked Jan Ch'iu of Confucius, 'that we can ever know of the origin of the universe?'

'Why, yes,' replied Confucius, 'the time of long ago is just like the present.'

Jan Ch'iu did not know what to say and withdrew. The next day, he came again and said, 'Yesterday I asked you if we could know the origin of the universe and you said, "Yes, the time of long ago is like the present." Yesterday I seemed to understand what you mean, but today, I feel in the dark. Will you please enlighten me?'

'You understood my meaning yesterday,' replied Confucius, 'because you were in full possession of your spirit. And now you are in the dark because you have lost it and are trying to find it. There is no such thing as long ago and the present, or the beginning and the end. Is it possible to have children and grandchildren before you have children and grandchildren?'

Before Jan Ch'iu was able to reply, Confucius continued. 'I see you cannot reply. Do not consider death as arising from life and do not consider life as dying with death. Both life and death are dependent on something else and find their unity elsewhere. Do you suppose that there was something which existed before the origin of the universe? That something which gives birth to other things could not be a thing itself, for things could not exist before there was something. There must have been something else which preceded it and there must have been something which still preceded that preceding something.'(6:4)

See also selection 2.3.
'All things come from not being.' See selection I.4.

BOOK FIVE

THE CONDUCT OF LIFE

41. QUALITIES OF THE TAOIST

When the highest type of men hear the Tao (truth),
   They try hard to live in accordance with it,
When the mediocre type hear the Tao,
   They seem to be aware and yet unaware of it.
When the lowest type hear the Tao,
   They break into loud laughter-
   If it were not laughed at, it would not be Tao.

Therefore there is the established saying:
   'Who understands Tao seems dull of comprehension;
   Who is advanced in Tao seems to slip backwards;

Who moves on the even Tao (Path) seems to go up and down.'

Superior character appears like a hollow (valley);
Sheer white appears like tarnished;
Great character appears like insufficient;
Solid character appears like infirm;
Pure worth appears like contaminated.
   Great space has no corners;
   Great talent takes long to mature;
   Great music is faintly heard;
   Great form has no contour
   And Tao is hidden without a name.
It is this Tao that is adept at lending (its power) and bringing fulfilment.

The philosophic basis of Lao tzu's and Chuang tzu's thoughts has been entirely covered in the preceding four books. From here on, Lao tzu's Book of Tao seems to deal principally with the practical applications of his philosophy, a fact which seems to justify an ancient division of the book into two hales. The first book, Chapters 1 to 37, was called the Book of Tao, and the second book, Chapters 38 to 81, was called the Book of Teh. After a careful study of the chapters, I have come to the conclusion that if such a division into two books is to be made, marking the two parts dealing with principles and their application respectively, it should be made at this point, particularly because Chapter 40 gives the best summary of Lao tzu's philosophy.

Chuang tzu's most important philosophic ideas have already been given in the preceding pages, with two exceptions. First, Chuang tzu's most beautiful writings deal with the problem of life and death, which I have arranged under Chapter so. Second, Chuang tzu's theory of knowledge and its limitations is further developed in Chapter s6. These two are important chapters for the study of Chuang tzu's thought.

The theme of Chapters 41-46 is contentment and the reality or unreality of gain and loss. An ancient editor, Wu Ch'eng, combined Chapters 41, 42, 43 into one, as he did with several other groups of chapters. His regrouping of chapters generally makes for better continuity of thought.

41.1. 'SHEER WHITE APPEARS LIKE TARNISHED; GREAT CHARACTER APPEARS LIKE INSUFFICIENT.'
Yang Tsechu(Yang Chu)went down south to see the city of P'ei. At this time, Lo Tan(Lao tzu) was travelling west to Ch'in and Yang Chu made an appointment to see him in the suburb, and they met each other at Liang. When Lao tzu saw Yang on the road, he turned his head to the sky and sighed, saying, 'I thought you could be my disciple. Now I know you cannot.'

Yang Tsechu did not reply. When they arrived, they were served with a basin of water and towels and left their shoes outside the door. Yang Chu went forward on his knees and aid, 'I was going to ask you something, Master, but you were occupied on the road, and I did not dare. Now you are free.May I ask what is my fault?'

'You have that haughty look. Who would want to be in the same room with you? Sheer white appears like tarnished; great character appears like insufficient.'

Yang Tsechu changed his countenance and said, 'Thank you for your advice.'

Now when Yangtse left his house to see Lao tzu, the people in the house used to make way for him. An old man held the mat for him and his wife held the comb and towels ready. The other people in the house left the mat, and the cook left the stove to make way for him. When he returned (after seeing Lao tzu), the people in the house mingled freely with him on the mat. (7:10)

In the Prolegomena, this quotation from Lao tzu is given as, 'Be aware of the white, but keep to the tarnished.'

42. THE VIOLENT MAN

Out of Tao, One is born;
Out of One, Two;
Out of Two, Three;
Out of Three, the created universe.
The created universe carries the *yin* at its back and the *yang* in front;
Through the union of the pervading principles it reaches harmony.
To be 'orphaned,' 'lonely' and 'unworthy' is what men hate most.
Yet the princes and dukes call themselves by such names
For sometimes things are benefited by being taken away from,
And suffer by being added to.

Others have taught this maxim,
Which I shall teach also:
'The violent man shall die a violent death.'
This I shall regard as my spiritual teacher.

42.1. 'OUT OF TAO, ONE IS BORN'
'Since I can say the word One, how can speech not exist? If it does exist, we have One and speech-two; two and one-three, from which point on, even the best mathematicians will fail to reach (the ultimate).' *See selection 2.3.*

On the operation of *yin* and *yang*, see selection 25.1, 'The Mystery of the Universe,' and 25.2, 'The eternal cycle.'

43. THE SOFTEST SUBSTANCE

The softest substance of the world
Goes through the hardest.
That-which-is-without-form penetrates that-which-has-no-crevice
Through this I know the benefit of taking no action.[1]
The teaching without words
And the benefit of taking no action
    Are without compare in the universe.

1 Pervading influence of the spirit reaches everywhere, in contrast with superficial activities which create obstacles of their own.

43.1.'THAT WHICH IS WITHOUT FORM PENETRATES THAT WHICH HAS NO CREVICE.' THE PARABLE OF THE BUTCHER.
Prince Huei's cook was cutting up a bullock. Every blow of his hand, every heave of his shoulders, every tread of his foot, every thrust of his knee, every *whshh* of rent flesh, every *chhk* of the chopper, was in perfect rhythm-like the dance of the *Mulberry Grove*, like the harmonious chords of *Chine Shou*.

'well done!' cried the Prince. 'Yours is skill indeed !'

'Sire,' replied the cook laying down his chopper, 'I have always devoted myself to Tao, which is higher than mere skill. When I first began to cut up bullocks, I saw before me whole bullocks. After three years' practice, I saw no more whole animals. And now I work with my mind and not with my eye. My mind works along without the control of the senses. Falling back upon eternal principles, I glide through such great joints or cavities as there may be, according to the natural constitution of the animal. I do not even touch the convolutions of muscle and tendon, still less attempt to cut through large bones.

'A good cook changes his chopper once a year-because he cuts. An ordinary cook, once a month--because he hacks. But I have had this chopper nineteen years, and although I have cut up many thousand bullocks, its edge is as if fresh from the whetstone. For at the joints there are always interstices, and the edge of a chopper being without thickness, it remains only to insert that which is without thickness into such an interstice. Indeed there is plenty of room for the blade to move about. It is thus that I have kept my chopper for nineteen years as though fresh from the whetstone.

'Nevertheless, when I come upon a knotty part which is difficult to tackle, I am all caution. Fixing my eye on it, I stay my hand, and gently apply my blade, until with a *hwah* the part yields like earth crumbling to the ground. Then I take out my chopper and stand up, and look around, and pause with an air of triumph. Then wiping my chopper, I put it carefully away.'

'Bravo!' cried the Prince. 'From the words of this cook I have learnt how to take care of my life.'[2]

2 In the translation of this passage I follow mainly that by H. A. Giles, with certain minor changes.

On the 'Doctrine without words,' see Chapters 2 and 56. Chuang tzu explains it on the basis of the inadequacy of language to convey what we mean.

44. BE CONTENT

Fame or one's own self, which does one love more?
One's own self or material goods, which has more worth?
Loss (of self) or possession (of goods), which is the greater evil?

Therefore: he who loves most spends most,
    He who hoards much loses much.
The contented man meets no disgrace;
Who knows when to stop runs into no danger-
He can long endure.

44.1. CHUANG TZU WAS IN A PARK. Chuang Chou (Chuang tzu) was one day wandering within the confines of the Tiao park, when he saw a strange bird coming from the south. Its wingspread was seven feet across, and its eyes were an inch in circumference. The bird's wing touched his forehead and it flew on to rest in a chestnut grove. 'What kind of a bird is this?' said Chuang tzu to himself. 'With its big wings it does not fly away, and with its big eyes it does not see.' So he picked up his skirt and ran along and watched it with a sling in his hand. He saw a cicada enjoying itself in the shade, forgetting itself. Behind it was a praying mantis taking advantage of the shadow to pounce upon it. The praying mantis also forgot himself in the love of game, for the strange bird was behind him. The bird in turn was attracted by gain, and forgot himself. (As Chuang Chou was going to shoot the bird,) he suddenly drew up and said to himself, 'Alas! This is the manner in which things involve one another and loss follows upon gain.'

Chuang Chou threw away his sling and started to return when the park keeper saw him and drove him away with angry words. Chuang Chou returned to his house and remained unhappy for three days.

'Why are you so unhappy?' asked Lin Chu (his disciple)

'I got so occupied with the corporeal things that I forgot myself. Looking upon the muddy stream, I forgot the deep clear pool. I have heard from the Master (Lao tzu), "When you enter a country, follow its customs." I was wandering in the Tiao park and forgot myself. The strange bird touched my forehead and forgot itself in the chestnut grove. The keeper of the chestnut grove took me for a thief. That is why I am feeling unhappy.' (5:II)

44.2. ON LOSING ONE'S REAL SELF. He who pursues fame at the risk of losing his self is not a scholar. He who loses his life and is not true to himself can never be a master of man. Thus Hu Puhsieh, Wu Kuang, Po Yi, Shu Ch'i, Chitse Hsuyü, Chi T'o, and Shent'u Ti, were kept busy in the service of others, and had the pleasure of pleasing others, but never the pleasure of pleasing themselves. (2:5)

44.3. CONFUCIUS RECEIVED ADVICE FROM A TAOIST.

Confucius spoke to Tsesanghu, 'I have been driven twice from Lu. My tree was cut down in Sung. I had to hide myself in Wei. I got into trouble in Shang and Chou, and was in hiding in the plains between Ch'en and Ts'ai. After these successive troubles, my friends are deserting me and my disciples are beginning to go away. Tell me, what is the trouble with me?'

'Haven't you heard of how the man of Chia fled his country?' replied Tsesanghu. 'When Lin Huei fled, he abandoned his piece of jade which was worth a thousand dollars, and carried his child on his back. Someone said to him, "I cannot imagine that you are trying to save the cloth on the child's back, for the cloth is not worth much. As for avoiding trouble, the child will only give you more trouble than the jade. Why do you abandon the jade of a thousand dollars and flee with your child on your back?" And Lin Huei replied, "I value the jade because of its material value, but the child is my natural kin." Those who come together for profit or gain abandon each other in times of trouble. Those who belong together by nature help one another in times of distress. What a difference there is between the two. The friendship between gentlemen is mild like the taste of water; the friendship between petty people is sweet like strong wine. But the gentle men's mild friendship develops into lasting affection, and the petty people's friendship begins with sweetness and ends with breaking off. For those who come together without a natural reason also break away from one another without a natural reason.'

'Thank you for your advice,' replied Confucius. He slowly strode away and returned to his home. He threw away all his books and stopped his studies. The disciples could not learn anything from him and they grew in their affection for their master. (5:9)

44.4. THOSE WHO UNDERSTAND LIFE. Those who understand life do not occupy themselves with things that are of no benefit to life. Those who understand destiny do not occupy themselves with what cannot be helped in the realm of knowledge. One depends on material means to strengthen the body, but there are plenty of people who have more than enough of the material means and yet whose bodies are not strong. One cannot live without taking care of the body, yet there are plenty of people who do take care of their bodies and lose their lives. Alas! We can control neither birth nor death. The people of this world think that they can preserve life by taking care of their bodies, but if they cannot preserve their lives by taking care of their bodies, then what are they so busy about? To attend to things which are not worth attending to but which have to be attended to is no escape. Those who wish to escape living for their bodies should not attend to business affairs. Those who do not attend to business affairs have no entanglements. Disentanglement means calm and repose; calm and repose mean the beginning of the new life, and when one begins a new life, he comes near to Tao. Business affairs are not worth forgetting and this life is not worth abandoning. By forsaking business affairs, one's body is relieved from worry, and by abandoning life, one's spirit is preserved whole. When a man's body is at ease, and his spirit is recovered, he becomes One with heaven. The heaven and earth are the parents of the things of the universe. When the spirit is united with matter, the body is formed; when the spirit departs, it returns to the origin of things. (5:3)

There are three or four anecdotes about Chuang tzu recorded in his works, showing his contempt for government office, of which two are given below.

44.5. CHUANG TZU REFUSED GOVERNMENT OFFICE. Chuang tzu was fishing on the P'u River when the Prince of Ch'u sent two high officials to see him and said, 'Our Prince desires to burden you with the administration of the Ch'u State.'

Chuang tzu went on fishing without turning his head and said, 'I have heard that in Ch'u there is a sacred tortoise which died when it was three thousand (years) old. The prince keeps this tortoise carefully enclosed in a chest in his ancestral temple. Now would this tortoise rather be dead and have its remains venerated, or would it rather be alive and wagging its tail in the mud?'

'It would rather be alive,' replied the two officials, 'and wagging its tail in the mud.'

'Begone!' cried Chuang tzu. 'I too will wag my tail in the mud.'

Hueitse was Prime Minister in the Liang State, and Chuang tzu was on his way to see him.

Someone remarked, 'Chuang tzu has come. He wants to be minister in your place.'

Thereupon Hueitse was afraid, and searched all over the country for three days and three nights to find him.

Then Chuang tzu went to see him, and said, 'Do you know there is a bird in the south which is a kind of phoenix? When it starts to fly from the South Sea to the North Sea, it will not alight except on the *wu-t'ung* tree. It eats nothing but the fruit of the bamboo, drinks nothing but the purest spring water. An owl which has got a rotten mouse looks up as the phoenix flies by, and screeches. Are you screeching at me for fear of losing your premiership?' (4:15)

45. CALM QUIETUDE

The highest perfection is like imperfection,[3]
    And its use is never impaired.
The greatest abundance seems meagre,
    And its use will never fail.
What is most straight appears devious,
The greatest skill appears like clumsiness;
The greatest eloquence seems like stuttering.
Movement overcomes cold,
(But) keeping still overcomes heat.
Who is calm and quiet becomes the guide for the universe.

3 Because it assumes fluid form according to circumstances.

'The highest perfection is like imperfection' --*see Chuang tzu's saying in selection 2.1: 'Division is the same as creation; creation is the same as destruction. There is no such thing as creation or destruction, for the conditions are again levelled together into One.'*

'The greatest skill appears like clumsiness' --*see selection 19.1 where the same line in identical wording is given as a quotation.*

'The greatest eloquence seems like stuttering' --*see Chuang tzu's saying to identical effect in selection 2.3: 'Therefore, it is said that one who argues does so because he is confused. ... a perfect argument does not employ words.'*

'Who is calm and quiet becomes the guide for the universe' --*see the development of this idea in almost identical phraseology in the important selections 37.I and 37.2.*

46. RACING HORSES

When the world lives in accord with Tao,
Racing horses are turned back to haul refuse carts.
When the world lives not in accord with Tao,
Cavalry abounds in the countryside.

There is no greater curse than the lack of contentment.
No greater sin than the desire for possession.
Therefore he who is contented with contentment shall be always content.

The present chapter provides perhaps the best illustration of the fact that the so-called 'chanters' in Lao tzu's book often consist of his sayings on unrelated topics. The preceding chapter is also a case in point. It is almost certain that the division into chapters was not original with Lao tzu, and that it was made by some editor at a very early date.

I have pointed out in the preface that Chuang tzu has very little to say about contentment, probably because he was not the type of man to preach this virtue. He also had very little to say about the most important ethical virtue taught by Lao tzu, namely, humility. Where Lao tzu spoke of contentment, Chuang tzu spoke about contempt for material power and wealth. I have been able to find in the entire works of Chuang tzu only one or two lines which may strictly be interpreted as an advice on contentment.

46.1. THE TIT.
The tit, building its nest in the mighty forest, occupies but a single twig. The beaver slakes its thirst from the river, but drinks enough only to fill its belly. (I:2)

47. PURSUIT OF KNOWLEDGE
Without stepping outside one's doors,
    One can know what is happening in the world,
Without looking out of one's windows,
    One can see the Tao of Heaven.

The farther one pursues knowledge,
    The less one knows.
Therefore the Sage knows without running about,
    Understands without seeing,
    Accomplishes without doing.

There is some basis in Lao tzu's works, and considerably more in Chuang tzu's, for the later development of Taoism into a study of popular witchcraft and spiritism. Such teachings were based on the idea of the conquest of mind over matter. The present chapter, for instance, gives a suggestion of that mystical twist. See also the last part of Chapter 50 and Chapter 59. Lao tzu himself said only a few words about the art of escaping death and becoming an immortal, which form is the main body of later Taoist legends. But in Chuang tzu and still more in Liehtse the Chinese believers of the occult world found many teachings to justify their belief. The following is an example of early yoga teaching.

47.1. CONFUCIUS ON THE 'FASTING OF THE HEART.'
(CONEUCIUS ADVISED HIS DISCIPLE YEN HUEI TO KEEP FAST.)
   'My family is poor,' replied Yen Huei, 'and for many months we have tasted neither wine nor flesh. Is that not fasting?'

   'That is a fast according to the religious observances,' answered Confucius, 'but not the fasting of the heart.'
   'And may I ask,' said Yen Huei, 'in what consists the fasting of the heart?'
   'Concentrate your will. Hear not with your ears, but with your mind; not with your mind, but with your spirit. Let your hearing stop with the ears, and let your mind stop with its images. Let your spirit, however, be like a blank, passively responsive to externals. In such open receptivity only can Tao abide. And that open receptivity is the fasting of the heart.'
   'Then,' said Yen Huei, 'the reason I cannot use this method is because of consciousness of a self. If I could apply this method, the assumption of a self would be gone. Is this what you mean by the receptive state?'
   'Exactly so,' replied the Master. 'Let me tell you ...
   'Look at that emptiness. There is brightness in an empty room. Good luck dwells in repose. If there is not (inner) repose, your mind will be galloping about though you are sitting still. Let your ears and eyes communicate within but shut out all knowledge from the mind.' (1:13)

48. CONQUERING THE WORLD BY INACTION

The student of knowledge (aims at) learning day by day;
The student of Tao (aims at) losing day by day.
   By continual losing
   One reaches doing nothing (*laissez-faire*).
   By doing nothing everything is done.
He who conquers the world often does so by doing nothing.[4]
When one is compelled to do something,[5]
The world is already beyond his conquering.

4 By moral influence.
5 By ordering people about.

'The student of knowledge aims at learning day by day; the student of Tao aims at losing day by day. By continual losing, one reaches doing nothing. By doing nothing, everything is done.'- *The entire quotation is given in identical wording as a quotation in Chuang tzu, 6:1.*

The doctrine of inaction is usually difficult to understand. Interpreted in the light of science, it means making use of the natural forces to achieve one's object with the greatest economy. The best saying of Chuang tzu to this effect is given in the form of an illustration. 'For a fire-man to feed the fire by adding one log to another by hand, there is a limit. But for the fire to spread by itself, the process is continuous.' (I:II) Se also the 'Parable of the butcher' in selection 43.1.

49. THE PEOPLE'S HEARTS

The Sage has no decided opinions and feelings,[6]
But regards the people's opinions and feelings as his own.

The good ones I declare good;
The bad ones I also declare good.
   That is the goodness of Virtue.

The honest ones I believe;
The liars I also believe;
   That is the faith of Virtue.
The Sage dwells in the world peacefully, harmoniously.
The people of the world are brought into a community of heart,
And the Sage regards them all as his own children.

> 6 Hsin, lit. 'heart.' Both thinking and feeling are denoted by this word. It is impossible to say a 'decided heart.'

   Both Lao tzu and Chuang tzu taught that the wise ruler, who must let the people decide things for themselves and live their natural life, should not have definite opinions of his own, but should guide himself by the opinions of the people.

49.1. 'THE SAGE REGARDS THE PEOPLE'S OPINIONS AND FEELINGS AS HIS OWN.' The people of this world are pleased when people agree with them and displeased when people disagree. The fact that they like those who agree and dislike those who differ in their opinions shows that they think they are better than the others. But can those who think they are better than others be really better than others? Rather than hold one's own opinion against the many, let the many represent the many. But those who desire to govern kingdoms clutch at the advantages of (the systems of) the Three Kings without seeing the troubles involved. In fact, they are trusting the fortunes of a country to luck, but what country would be lucky enough to escape destruction? Their chances of preserving it do not amount to one in ten thousand, while their chances of destroying it are ten thousand to nothing and even more. Such, alas! is the ignorance of rulers. (3:8)

49.2. FOLLOWING THE PEOPLE. That which is low, but must be let alone, is matter. That which is humble, but still must be followed, is the people. (3:9)

50. THE PRESERVING OF LIFE

Out of life, death enters.
The companions (organs) of life are thirteen;⁷
The companions (organs) of death are (also) thirteen.
What send man to death in this life are also (these) thirteen.
How is it so?
Because of the intense activity of multiplying life.

It has been said that he who is a good preserver of his life
Meets no tigers or wild buffaloes on land,
Is not vulnerable to weapons in the field of battle.
The horns of the wild buffalo are powerless against him;
The paws of the tiger are useless against him;
The weapons of the soldier cannot avail against him.
    How is it so?
Because he is beyond death.⁸

> 7 According to Han Fei, the four limbs and nine external cavities. Another orthodox reading is 'three-tenths,' but this makes less sense.
> 8 Lit. 'deathless.'

What was philosophy in Lao tzu often became poetry in the younger Taoist disciple. If Lao tzu felt the pathos of human life and the mystery of death, he said very little about it. On the other hand, Chuang tzu felt the sorrow of man's short life on this earth and was fascinated by the mystery of death, and he constantly expressed this feeling with the gifted pen of a poet. I have collected here some of Chuang tzu's most beautiful writings which all happen to deal with the topic of life and death.

50.1. LIFE IS THE COMPANION OF DEATH, AND DEATH IS THE

BEGINNING OF LIFE. Who can appreciate the connection between the two? When a man is born, it is but the embodiment of a spirit. When the spirit is embodied, there is life, and when the spirit disperses, there is death. But if life and death are companions to each other, why should I be concerned? Therefore,all things are one. What we love is the mystery of life. What we hate is corruption in death. But the corruptible in its turn becomes mysterious life, and this mysterious life once more becomes corruptible. (6:1)

50.2. THE AGITATIONS OF MAN's SOUL. For whether the soul is locked in sleep or whether in waking hours the body moves,we are striving and struggling with the immediate circumstances. Some are easy-going and leisurely, some are deep and cunning, and some are secretive. Now we are frightened over petty fears, now disheartened and dismayed over some great terror. Now the mind flies forth like an arrow from a crossbow, to be the arbiter of right and wrong. Now it stays behind as if sworn to an oath, to hold on to what it has secured. Then,as under autumn and winter's blight, comes gradual decay, and submerged in its own occupations, it keeps on running its course, never to return. Finally, worn out and imprisoned, it is choked up like an old drain, and the failing mind shall not see light again.

Joy and anger, sorrow and happiness, worries and regrets,hesitation and fears, come upon us by turns, with ever-changing moods, like music from the hollows, or like mushrooms from damp. Day and night they alternate within us, but we cannot tell whence they spring. Alas! Alas! Could we for a moment lay our finger upon their very Cause?

But for these emotions I should not be. Yet but for me, there would be no one to feel them. So far we can go; but we do not know by whose order they come into play. It would seem there was a soul; but the clue to its existence is wanting. That it functions is credible enough, though we cannot see its form.Perhaps it has inner reality without outward form.

Take the human body with all its hundred bones, nine external cavities and six internal organs, all complete. Which part of it should I love best? Do you not cherish all equally, or have you a preference? Do these organs serve as servants of someone else? Since servants cannot govern themselves, do they serve as master and servants by turn? Surely there is some soul which controls them all.

But whether or not we ascertain what is the true nature of this soul, it matters but little to the soul itself. For once coming into this material shape, it runs its course until it is exhausted. To be harassed by the wear and tear of life, and to be driven along without possibility of arresting one's course-is not this pitiful indeed? To labour without cease all life, and then, without living to enjoy the fruit, worm out with labour, to depart, one knows not whither-is not this a just cause for grief?

Men say there is no death--of what avail? The body decomposes, and the mind goes with it. Is this not a great cause for sorrow? Is human life indeed such a puzzle? Or is it I alone who am puzzled, and others not so? (1:4, 5)

50.3. THOSE WHO DREAM OF THE BANQUET WAKE UP TO LAMENTATION AND SORROW.

How do I know that love of life is not a delusion after all? How do I know but that he who dreads death is not as a child who has lost his way and does not know his way home?

The lady Li Chi was the daughter of the frontier officer of Ai. When the Duke of Chin first got her, she wept until the bosom of her dress was drenched with tears. But when she came to the royal residence, shared with the Duke his luxurious couch, and ate rich food, she repented of having wept. How then do I know but that the dead may repent of having previously clung to life?

Those who dream of the banquet, wake to lamentation and sorrow. Those who dream of lamentation and sorrow wake to join the hunt. While they dream, they do not know that they are dreaming. Some will even interpret the very dream they are dreaming; and only when they awake do they know it was a dream. By and by comes the great awakening, and then we find out that this life is really a great dream. Fools think they are awake now, and flatter themselves they know-this one is a prince, and that one is a shepherd. What narrowness of mind! Confucius and you are both dreams; and I who say you are dreams-I am but a dream myself. This is a paradox.Tomorrow a Sage may arise to explain it; but that tomorrow will not be until ten thousand generations have gone by. Yet you may meet him around the corner.

'The pure men of old did not know what it was to love life or to hate death.' *See selection 15.1.*

50.4. HUMAN LIFE IS SHORT. Human life in this world is but as the form of a white pony flashing across a rock crevice. In a moment it is gone. Suddenly waking up, all life is born; suddenly slipping off, all silently creep away. With one change,one is born; with another, one dies. Living creatures moan, and mankind weeps. Remove its bondage, slip off its skin-carcass,and curling up, where shall the soul of man[9] go and the body go with it? Is it perhaps on the great journey home?

9 The Chinese conception of the soul divides it into two kinds, hwen, which corresponds to the conscious mind, and p' o, which corresponds to the deep unconscious,according to C. G.Jung's interpretation of these two Chinese words in 'The Secret of the Golden Flower.'

50.5. MENGSUN'S DEATH. THE SHLE MAY BE A DREAM. Yen Huei said to Chungni (Confucius), 'When Mengsun Ts'ai's mother died, he wept, but without snivelling; his heart was not grieved; he wore mourning but without sorrow. Yet although wanting in these three points, he is considered the best mourner in the State of Lu. Can there be really people with a hollow reputation? I am astonished.'

'Mr Menesun.' said Chungni, 'has really mastered (the Tao). He has gone beyond the wise ones. There are still some things he cannot quite give up, but he has already given up certain things. Mr Mengsun knows not whence we come in life nor whither we go in death. He knows not which to put first and which to put last. He is ready to be transformed into other things without caring into what he may be transformed-that is all. How could that which is changing say that it will not change, and how could that which regards itself as permanent realize that it is changing already? Even you and I are perhaps dreamers who have not yet awakened. Moreover, he know his form is subject to change, but his mind remains the same. He believes not in real death, but regards it as moving into a new house. He weeps only when he sees others weep, as it comes to him naturally.

'Besides, we all talk of "me." How do you know what is this "me" that we speak of? You dream you are a bird, and soar to heaven, or dream you are a fish, and dive into the ocean's depths. And you cannot tell whether the man now speaking is awake or in a dream.

'A man feels a pleasurable sensation before he smiles, and smiles before he thinks how he ought to smile. Resign yourself to the sequence of things, forgetting the changes of life, and you shall enter into the pure, the divine, the One.'

50.6. CHUANG TZU DREAMING OF BEING A BUTTERFLY.

Once upon a time, I, Chuang Chou, dreamt I was a butterfly, fluttering hither and thither, to all intents and purposes a butterfly. I was conscious only of my happiness as a butterfly, unaware that I was Chou. Soon I awakened, and there I was, veritably myself again. Now I do not know whether I was then a man dreaming I was a butterfly, or whether I am now a butterfly, dreaming I am a man. Between a man and a butterfly there is necessarily a distinction. The transition is called the transformation of material things.[10]

[10] An important idea that recurs frequently in Chuang tzu: all things are in constant flux and change, but are different aspects of the One.

50.7. KUANGCH'ENGTSE ON BECOMING AN IMMORTAL.

The Yellow Emperor sat on the throne for nineteen years, and his laws obtained all over the empire. Hearing that Kuangch'engtse was living on Mount K'ungt'ung, he went there to see him, and said, 'I am told that you are in possession of perfect Tao. May I ask what is its essence? I desire to obtain the essence of the universe to secure good harvests and feed my people, and control the *yin* and *yang* principles to fulfil the life of all living things.'

'What you are asking about,' replied Kuangch'engtse, 'is merely the substance of matter. What you wish to control are the remnant forms. Ever since the empire was governed by you, the clouds have rained before thickening, the foliage of trees has fallen before turning yellow, and the brightness of the sun and moon has increasingly paled. You have the shallowness of mind of a glib talker. How then are you fit to speak of perfect Tao?'

The Yellow Emperor withdrew. He resigned the Throne. He built himself a solitary hut, and sat upon white straw. For three months he remained in seclusion, and then went again to see Kuangch'engtse.

The latter was lying with his head towards the south. The Yellow Emperor approached from below upon his knees. Kowtowing twice upon the ground, he said, 'I am told that you are in possession of perfect Tao. May I ask how to order one's life so that one may have long life?'

Kuang Ch'engtse jumped up with a start. 'A good question indeed!' cried he. 'Come, and I will speak to you of perfect Tao. The essence of perfect Tao is profoundly mysterious; its extent is lost in obscurity.

'See nothing; hear nothing; guard your spirit in quietude and your body will go right of its own accord. Be quiet, be pure; abuse not your body, perturb not your vital essence, and you will live for ever. For if the eye sees nothing, and the ear hears nothing, and the mind thinks nothing, your spirit will stay in your body, and the body will thereby live for ever. Cherish that which is within you, and shut off that which is without; for much knowledge is a curse.

'Then I will take you to that abode of Great Light to reach the Plateau of Absolute *Yang*. I will lead you through the Door of the Dark Unknown to the Plateau of the Absolute *Yin*.

'The Heaven and Earth have their separate functions. The *yin* and *yang* have their hidden root. Guard carefully your body, and material things will prosper by themselves. I guard the One, and rest in harmony with externals. Therefore I have been able to live for twelve hundred years and my body has not grown old.'

The Yellow Emperor kowtowed twice and said, 'Kuangch'engtse is surely God....'

'Come, said Kuangch'engtse, 'I will tell you. Men regard as mortal that which is eternal, and consider as finite that which is infinite. Those who possess my Tao are princes in this life and rulers in the hereafter. Those who do not possess my Tao behold the light of day in this life and become clods of earth in the hereafter.

'Nowadays, all living things spring from the dust and to the dust return. But I will lead you through the portals of Eternity to wander in the great wilds of Infinity. My light is the light of sun and moon. My life is the life of Heaven and Earth. Before me all is nebulous; behind me all is dark, unknown. Men may all die, but I endure for ever.' (3:7)

50.8. WHY THE MAN OF TAO IS BEYOND ALL HARM.

'If this is the case,' said the Spirit of the River, 'what is the value of Tao?'

'Those who understand Tao,' answered the Spirit of the Ocean, 'must necessarily apprehend the eternal principles and those who apprehend the eternal principles must understand their application. Those who understand their application do not suffer material things to injure them.

'The man of perfect character cannot be burnt by fire, nor drowned by water, nor hurt by the cold of winter or the heat of summer, nor torn by bird or beast. Not that he makes light of these; but that he discriminates between safety and danger, is happy under prosperous and adverse circumstances alike, and cautious in his choice of action, so that none can harm him.'

51. THE MYSTIC VIRTUE

Tao gives them birth,
Teh (character) fosters them.
The material world gives them form.
The circumstances of the moment complete them.
Therefore all things of the universe worship Tao and exalt Teh.
Tao is worshiped and Teh is exalted
Without anyone's order but is so of its own accord.

Therefore Tao gives them birth,
Teh fosters them,
Makes them grow, develops them,
Gives them a harbour, a place to dwell in peace,
Feeds them and shelters them.
   It gives them birth and does not own them,
   Acts (helps) and does not appropriate them,
   Is superior, and does not control them.
   --This is the Mystic Virtue.

   'The things of the creation are nourished by it, without knowing it. This is the root, from which one may survey the universe.' *See selection 6.1.*
   '(Tao) acts and does not appropriate them, is superior and does not control them.' *These lines are given as a quotation in Chuang tzu 5:7.*

52. STEALING THE ABSOLUTE

There was a beginning of the universe
   Which may be regarded as the Mother of Universe.
From the Mother, we may know her sons.
   After knowing the sons, keep to the Mother.
   Thus one's whole life may be preserved from harm.

Stop its apertures,
Close its doors,

And one's whole life is without toil.

Open its apertures,
Be busy about its affairs,
And one's whole life is beyond redemption.

He who can see the small is clear-sighted;
He who stays by gentility is strong.
   Use the light,
   And return to clear-sightedness-
Thus cause not yourself later distress.
--This is to rest in the Absolute.

   In this chapter the 'mother' refers to Tao, the source of all things, and her 'sons' refer to the things of the universe, which are Tao in its manifested forms. By recognising that all things of the universe come from the same source and by keeping to the unity, one achieves an emancipation of spirit which overcomes the individuality of things.

52.1. ON KNOWING AND NOT KNOWING THE ONENESS OF THINGS. Only the truly intelligent understand this principle of the levelling of all things into One.... But to wear out one's intellect in an obstinate adherence to the individuality of things, not recognising the fact that all things are One-this is called 'Three in the Morning.' What is 'Three in the Morning?' A keeper of monkeys said with regard to their rations of nuts that each monkey was to have three in the morning and four at night. At this the monkeys were very angry. Then the keeper said they might have four in the morning and three at night, with which arrangement they were all well pleased. The actual number of nuts remained the same, but there was a difference owing to (subjective evaluations of) likes and dislikes. It also derives from this (principle of subjectivity). Wherefore the true Sage brings all the contraries together and rests in the natural Balance of Heaven. This is called (the principle of following) two courses (at once).

52.2. TAO UNIFIES THE PARTS. Tao unifies the parts. In creation there is destruction. The disadvantage of regarding things in their separate parts is that when one begins to cutup and analyse,each one tries to be exhaustive. The disadvantage of trying to be exhaustive is that it is consciously (mechanically) exhaustive.One goes on deeper and deeper, forgetting to return, and sees a ghost (the externals of things only). Or one goes on and imagines he's got it, and what he has got is only a carcass. For a thing which retains its substance but has lost the magic touch of life is but a ghost (of reality). Only one who can imagine the formless in the formed can arrive at the truth. (6:8)

52.3. THE SAGE RESTS IN THE SOLUTION OF THINGS. The sage rests in the solution of things and is dissatisfied with what is not a solution. The common men are satisfied with what is not a solution and do not rest in what is a solution. (8:13)

53. BRIGANDAGE

If I were possessed of Austere Knowledge,
Walking on the Main Path (Tao),
I would avoid the by-paths.
   The Main Path is easy to walk on,
   Yet people love the small by-paths.

The (official) courts are spick and span,
(While) the fields go untilled,
And the (people's) granaries are very low.
(Yet) clad in embroidered gowns,
And carrying fine swords,
Surfeited with good food and drinks,
(They are) splitting with wealth and possessions.
-This is to lead the world towards brigandage.
   Is it not the corruption of Tao?

53.1. THINK FOR THE PIGS. A soothsayer put on his priest's garb and approached the pig pen. He spoke to the pigs, 'Do you hate to die? I shall feed you for three months, then fast you for ten days and segregate you for three days and then I shall put you on the sacrificial altar and cover your shoulders and haunches with white hay. What do you think of such a proposition?'

Then he thought that if he were in the pig's place, the pig would reply, 'I would rather that you would feed me with bran and leave me alone in the pig pen.'

But when a man plans for himself, he does not mind living with the honour and glory of badges and titles, and being put on a hearse inside its decorative arched cover. When a man thinks for the pig, he rejects such a proposition. But when he plans for himself, he accepts it. What difference is there between him and a pig? (5:5)

53.2. ON TRUE HAPPINESS. Is there such a thing as true happiness, or is there not? Is there such a thing which can preserve one's life, or is there not? What should I do and what should I believe? What should I avoid and what should I follow? What should I accept and what should I reject? What should I love and what should I hate? What the world values are wealth, rank, a long life and goodness. What people enjoy are good health, rich food, fine clothing, beauty and music. What they hate are poverty, a low position, dying young, and ugly disease. What people are worried about is that their body should not be in good health, that they might not be able to taste rich food, put on fine clothing, see beauty or hear good music. When they cannot obtain these things, they are plunged into deep sorrow and worry. Such attendance to the externals is indeed foolish. The rich hustle and bustle and hoard up wealth which they cannot use. Their method of attending to external comforts is superficial. Those in position plan and contrive day and night and ask, 'Shall I do this, or shan't I?' Their method of attending to the externals of life is undependable. When a man is born, sorrow comes with it. Those of old age live in senile decay, bound in sorrow, and yet they cannot die! What a sad picture! Are they not far gone astray in their pursuit of the visible things? Martyrs are in the world's opinion admittedly good. Yet their goodness does not prevent them from losing their life, and I do not know whether what is good is really good or bad. If the former, still it does not help them to preserve their lives; if the latter, still martyrdom enables them to save others....

As to what the world does and the way people seek happiness now, I do not know if such happiness be real happiness or unhappiness. I watch the world rushing about with the crowd to seek happiness, and see that something seems to drive them along. Yet they all say they are happy. I have not participated in their happiness or unhappiness. Is there, after all, such a thing as happiness or unhappiness?

I consider inaction as true happiness, while the world regards it as great misery. It has been said, 'Perfect happiness is the absence of (the striving for) happiness: perfect renown is the absence of (concern for) renown.' (5:1)

54. THE INDIVIDUAl AND THE STATE

Who is firmly established is not easily shaken.
Who has a firm grasp does not easily let go.
From generation to generation his ancestral sacrifices
    Shall be continued without fail.

Cultivated in the individual, character will become genuine;
Cultivated in the family, character will become abundant;
Cultivated in the village, character will multiply;
Cultivated in the state, character will prosper;
Cultivated in the world, character will become universal.

Therefore:
    According to (the character of) the individual, judge the individual;
    According to (the character of) the family, judge the family;
    According to (the character of) the village, judge the village;
    According to (the character of) the state, judge the state;
    According to (the character of) the world, judge the world.
    How do I know the world is so.
    By this.[11]

    11 From within myself; or the meaning could be very well developed in the following chapter, since the chapter division is arbitrary.

    The idea behind the first two lines is essential distrust of visible devices, stated more clearly in the beginning of Chapter 27. 'The precaution taken against thieves who open trunks, search bags, or ransack cabinets consists in securing with cord and fastening with bolts and locks. This is what the world calls wit. But a big thief comes along and carries off the cabinet on his shoulders, with box and bag, and runs away with them. His only fear is that the bolts and locks should not be strong enough.' *See selection 19.1.*

54.1. THE NINE TESTS OF CONFUCIUS FOR JUDGING MEN.

'Man's mind,' says Confucius, 'is more treacherous than mountains and rivers, and more difficult to know than the sky. For with the sky you know what to expect in respect of the coming of spring, summer, autumn and winter, and the alternation of day and night. But man hides his character behind an inscrutable appearance. There are those who appear tame and self-effacing, but conceal a terrible pride. There are those who have some special ability but appear to be stupid. There are those who are compliant and yielding but always get their objective. Some are hard outside but soft inside, and some are slow without but impatient within. Therefore those who rush forward to do the righteous thing as if they were craving for it, drop it like something hot. Therefore (in the judgment of men) a gentleman sends a man to a distant mission in order to test his loyalty. He employs him nearby in order to observe his manners. He gives him a lot to do in order to judge his ability. He suddenly puts a question to him in order to test his knowledge and makes a commitment with him under difficult circumstances to test his ability to live up to his word. He trusts him with money in order to test his heart, and announces to him the coming of a crisis to test his integrity. He makes him drunk in order to see the inside of his character, and puts him in female company to see his attitude towards women. Submitted to these nine tests, a fool always reveals himself.' (8:14)

55. THE CHARACTER OF THE CHILD

Who is rich[12] in character
Is like a child.
   No poisonous insects sting him,
   No wild beasts attack him,
   And no birds of prey pounce upon him.
His bones are soft, his sinews tender, yet his grip is strong.
Not knowing the union of male and female, yet his organs are
   complete,

    Which means his vigour is unspoiled.
Crying the whole day, yet his voice never runs hoarse,
    Which means his (natural) harmony is perfect.
To know harmony is to be in accord with the eternal,
(And) to know eternity is called discerning.
(But) to improve upon life is called an ill-men;
To let go the emotions through impulse[13] is called assertiveness.
(For) things age after reaching their prime;
That (assertiveness) would be against Tao.
And he who is against Tao perishes young.[14]

12 Lit. 'thick,' 'heavy.'
13 Hsin, lit. 'mind,' or 'heart.'
14 The last three lines are almost a repetition of the last three lines of Chapter 30, where they more properly belong.

Some of Chuang tzu's favourite sayings touch upon 'the wholeness of nature,' 'the wholeness of character,' the wholeness of talent,' and, 'the wholeness of bodily form.' These ideas correspond to Lao tzu's idea of keeping the unspoiled nature or the source of power. Consequently, both philosophers use the new-born child and sometimes the new-born calf as a symbol of unspoiled innocence of character, com-parable to the wholeness of the character of the saint. Chuang tzu sometimes uses the example of an ugly or deformed person to show the contrast between imperfection of bodily for and perfection of the spirit.

55.1. WHOLENESS OF TALENT: UGLY T'O.

Duke Ai of the Lu State said to Confucius, 'In the Wei State there is an ugly person, named Ait'ai (Ugly) T'o. The men who have lived with him cannot stop thinking about him. Women who have seen him, would say to their parents, "Rather than be another man's wife, I would be this man's concubine." He has over a dozen concubines and is still taking more. He never tries to lead others, but only follows them. He wields no power of a ruler by which he may protect men's lives; he has no wealth by which to gratify their bellies, and is besides frightfully loathsome. He follows but does not lead, and his name is not known outside his own State. Yet men and women alike all seek his company. So there must be something in him that is different from other people. I sent for him, and saw that he was indeed frightfully ugly. Yet we had not been many months together before I began to see there was something in this man. A year had not passed before I began to trust him. As my government wanted a prime minister, I offered him the post. He looked sullenly before he replied and appeared indifferent as if he would much rather have declined. Perhaps he did not think me good enough for him! At any rate, I gave the post to him; but in a very short time he left me and went away. I grieved for him as for a lost friend, as though there were none left with whom I could enjoy having my kingdom. What manner of man is this?'

'When I was on a mission to the State of Ch'u,' replied Confucius, 'I saw a litter of young pigs sucking their dead mother. After a while they looked at her, and then all left the body and went off. For their mother did not look at them any more, nor did she seem any longer to be of their kind. What they loved was their mother; not the body which contained her, but that which made the body what it was. When a man is killed in battle, his coffin is not covered with a square canopy. A man whose leg has been cut off does not value a present of shoes. In each case, the original purpose of such things is gone. The concubines of the Son of Heaven do not cut their nails or pierce their ears. Those (servants) who are married have to live outside (the palace) and cannot be employed again. Such is the importance attached to preserving the body whole. How much more valued is one who has preserved his character whole?

'Now Ugly T'o is trusted without saying anything, is wanted without any accomplishments, and is offered the government of a country with the only fear that he might decline. Indeed he must be the one whose talents are perfect and whose character is without outward form!'(2:3)

55.2. WHOLENESS OF CHARACTER: THE FIGHTING COCK.

Chishengtse used to raise fighting cocks for the king. After ten days had passed. the king asked if his cock was ready for a fight.

'Not yet,' he replied. 'The cock is still very impulsive and haughty.'

After another ten days, the king asked again, and Chishengtse replied, 'Not yet. He still reacts to noises and shadows.'

After another ten days had passed, the king asked again and he replied, 'Not yet. His eyes still have an angry look, and he is full of fight.'

Another ten days passed and he said, 'it is about ready When he hears other cocks crow, he does not even react. You look at him, and he appears like a wooden cock. His character is whole now. No other cock will dare to fight him but will run away at first sight.' (5:6)

55.3. THE NEW-BORN CALF: THE ART OF CONCENTRATION.

Yeh Ch'ueh (an old teacher in Emperor Yao's time) asked P'i Yi about Tao, and P'i Yi replied, 'Keep correct your form, concentrate your vision, and the heavenly harmony will come to you. Control your mind, concentrate your thinking, and the spirit will come to reside in you. Teh shall be your clothing and Tao shall be your shelter. You will stare blankly like a new born calf and will not try to find out the reason.' (6:2)

55.4. THE SHADOW, THE BODY, AND THE SPIRIT.

The Penumbra said to the Umbra. 'At one moment you move: at another you are at rest. At one moment you sit down: at another you get up. Why this instability of purpose?' 'Perhaps I depend.' replied the Umbra, 'upon something which causes me to do as I do; and perhaps that something depends in turn upon something else which causes it to do as it does. Or perhaps my dependence is like (the unconscious movements) of a snake's scales or of a cicada's wings. How can I tell why I do one thing, or why I do not do another?' (1:10)

There is a more elaborate version of the same parable of a dialogue between the skirts of a shadow and the shadow. The former depends upon the latter. The later depends upon the bod, and the body itself is dependent upon the spirit which moves it. In the other version, the shadow says, 'I am like a snake's or a cicada's shredded skin, an empty form which resembles the body,' which seems an improvement upon the above version.

55.5. ON 'NOT IMPROVING UPON LIFE.'

(Says Chuang tzu) 'By a man without passions I mean one who does not permit likes and dislikes to disturb his internal economy, but rather falls in line with nature and does not try to improve upon (the materials of) living.' (2:5)

56. BEYOND HONOUR AND DISGRACE

He who knows does not speak;

He who speaks does not know.
　Fill up its apertures,
　Close its doors,
　Dull its edges,
　Untie its tangles,
　Soften its light,
　Submerge its turmoil,
　-This is the Mystic Unity.[15]
Then love and hatred cannot touch him.
Profit and loss cannot reach him.
Honour and disgrace cannot affect him.
Therefore is he always the honoured one of the world.

15 All submerged in the One.

56.1. 'HE WHO KNOWS DOES NOT SPEAK; HE WHO SPEAKS DOES NOT KNOW.' When people think of learning the truth, they think of books. Books are only words and words, of course, have a value. But the value of words lies in the meaning behind them. This co-called meaning is but an effort to grasp at something and that something cannot really be expressed by words. Because the world values words, it preserves the books.But I do not value them, because what they value is not the real value of the books. What the eye can see are form and colour. What the ear can hear are names and sounds. Alas! People think that from forms and colours, and names and sounds, they can penetrate to the truths of reality. Since form and colour and names and sounds cannot help one to penetrate to the truths of reality, therefore he who knows does not speak, and he who speaks does not know. But what does the world know about it?

　Duke Huan was reading in the hall and a cartwright was making a wheel in the yard in front. Laving down his chisel,he went up and spoke to Duke Huan.
　'May I ask what Your Royal Highness is reading?'
　'I am reading the works of the sages,' was the reply.
　'Are those sages living?'
　'No, they died long ago.'

'Then what you are reading is merely the chaff left over by the ancients.'

'I am reading,' said the King. 'What does a cart-wright know about things like books? Explain yourself. If you can give a good account of your remark, I shall let you go, and if not, you shall die.'

'Let me take an example from my own profession,' replied the carpenter. 'When I make the spokes too tight, they won't fit into the wheel, and when I make them too loose, they will not hold. I have to make them just right. I feel them with my hands and judge them with my heart. There is something about it which I cannot put down in words. I cannot teach that feeling to my own son, and my son cannot learn it from me. Therefore, at the age of seventy I am good at making wheels. The ancients perished long ago and that something which they could not communicate perished with them. Therefore. what Your Majesty is reading is the chaff of the ancients.'(4:4)

That form comes from the formless and the formless operates through form is understood by everybody. All people speak about this, but the man who understands Tao ignores such discussion. He who understands Tao finally does not discuss,and he who discusses does not understand Tao finally. (6:3)

56.2. IT'S DIFFICULT NOT TO TALK ABOUT TAO. Chuang tzu says, 'It is easy to know Tao, and difficult not to talk about it.To know and not to talk about it is to follow nature; to know and talk about it is to follow man. The ancients followed nature and did not follow man.' (8:13)

56.3. THE RELATIVITY OF KNOWLEDGE.

Yeh Ch'ueh asked Wang Yi, saying, 'Do you know for certain that all things are the same?'

'How can I know?' answered Wang Yi.

'Do you know what you do not know?'

'How can I know?' replied Wang Yi.

'But then does nobody know?'

'How can I know?' said Wang Yi. 'Nevertheless, I will try to tell you. How can it be known that what I call knowing is not really not knowing and that what I call not knowing is not really knowing? Now I would ask you this: If a man sleeps in a damp place, he gets lumbago and dies. But how about an eel? And living up in a tree is frightening and trying to one's nerves. But how about monkeys? Of the man, the eel, and the monkey, whose habitat is the right one, absolutely? Human beings feed on flesh, deer on grass,.centipedes on little snakes,owls and crows on mice. Of these four, whose is the right taste, absolutely? Monkey mates with the dog-headed female ape, the buck with the doe, eels consort with fishes, while men admire (the famous beauties) Mao Ch'iang and Li Chi, at the sight of whom fish plunge deep down in the water, birds soar high in the air, and deer hurry away. Yet who shall say which is the correct standard of beauty? In my opinion, the doctrines of humanity and justice and the paths of right and wrong are so confused that it is impossible to know their contentions.'

'If you, then,' asked Yeh Ch'ueh, 'do not know what is good and bad, is the Perfect Man equally without this knowledge?'

'The Perfect Man,' answered Wang Yi, 'is a spiritual being. Were the ocean itself scorched up, he would not feel hot. Were the great rivers frozen hard, he would not feel cold. Were the mountains to be cleft by thunder, and the great deep to be thrown up by storm, he would not tremble with fear. Thus, he would mount upon the clouds of heaven, and driving the sun and the moon before him, pass beyond the limits of his mundane existence. Death and life have no more victory over him. How much less should he concern himself with the distinctions of profit and loss?' (1:8)

'Then one who does not know really knows, and one who knows really does not know. Who knows this knowledge without knowing?' *See selection 1.1.*

56.4. THE MYSTIC VIRTUE. 'Cut down the activities of Tseng and Shih, pinch the mouths of Yang Chu and Motse, discard humanity and justice, and the character of the people will arrive at Mystic Unity.' *See selection 19.1.*

56.5. 'LOVE AND HATRED CANNOT TOUCH HIM; PROFIT AND LOSS CANNOT REACH HIM.' If the whole world flattered him, he would not be affected thereby, nor if the whole world blamed him would he be dissuaded from what he was doing. For Yung can distinguish between the inner and outer reality, and understand what is true honour and shame. (1:2)

The philosopher referred to here was Sung Yung. See the Prolegomena.

BOOK SIX

THE THEORY OF GOVERNMENT

57. THE ART OF GOVERNMENT

Rule a kingdom by the Normal.
Fight a battle by (abnormal) tactics of surprise.[1]
Win the world by doing nothing.
How do I know it is so?

Through this:
    The more prohibitions there are, the poorer the people become.
The more sharp weapons there are,
    The greater the chaos in the state.
The more skills of technique,
    The more cunning[2] things are produced.

The greater the number of statutes,
   The greater the number of thieves and brigands.
Therefore the Sage says:
I do nothing and the people are reformed[3] of themselves.
I love quietude and the people are righteous of themselves.
I deal in no business and the people grow rich by themselves.
I have no desires and the people are simple and honest by
   themselves.

1 Cheng, the normal, the straight, the righteous; ch'i, the abnormal, the deceitful, the surprising.
2 Ch'i, same word as that used for 'surprise tactics.'
3 Hua, touched, transformed, 'civilized' by moral influence. The best explanation of 'doing nothing.'

58. LAZY GOVERNMENT

When the government is lazy and dull,
   Its people are unspoiled;
When the government is efficient and smart,
   Its people are discontented.

Disaster is the avenue of fortune,
(And) fortune is the concealment for disaster.
   Who would be able to know its ultimate results?
(As it is), there would never be the normal,
   But the normal would (immediately) revert to the deceitful[4]
   And the good revert to the sinister.
Thus long has mankind gone astray!
Therefore the Sage is square (has firm principles), but not cutting (sharp-cornered),
Has integrity but does not hurt (others),[5]
Is straight, but not high-handed.
Bright, but not dazzling.

4 See Note 1.
5 In removing corruption by artificial laws and statutes and punishments.

The idea expressed in Chapters 57, 58, 59 and 60 is the danger of governmental interference with the people, and the chaos and confusion which have already been brought into the world by man's increase of knowledge. For a clearer view of the angry protests against the degeneration of man's character and the increase of cunning; and hypocrisy, cf. Chapters 18, 19, 28 and 38.

57.1. THE BAD INFLUENCE OF MACHINES.
Tsekung was travelling south to Ch'u and when he returned to Chin, he was passing Hanyin. There he met a peasant tending his vegetable garden. The peasant was dropping a bucket into the well and after he drew the water, he held the jar in his hand and went about to water his plants. All this involved a lot of labour with rather slow results.

'I know of a machine,' said Tsekung, 'which can irrigate a hundred fields in one day with great economy of labour and good results. Would you like to have a machine like that?'

The gardener looked up at him and said, 'What is it like?'

'It is a contrivance made of wood and the bar is weighted behind and light in front. It draws water up and the water comes flowing into a ditch gurgling in a steady, foamy stream. The machine is called a well-sweep.'

The peasant's face suddenly changed and he laughed. 'I have heard from my master,' he said, 'one who has cunning devices uses cunning in his affairs, and one who uses cunning in his affairs has cunning in his heart. When there is cunning in man's heart, he has lost something in him and becomes restless. With this restlessness of spirit, Tao will fly away. I knew all about the well-sweep, but I would be ashamed to use it.'

T'sekung felt abashed and he bent his head and did not say a thing. After a while, the gardener spoke, 'Who are you?'

'I am a disciple of Confucius,' was the reply.

'Are you not one of those people who read a lot of books to imitate the sages, who stretch and strive to benefit others and then play the string instrument alone and sing a sad song to sell their reputation to the world? If you could learn to do away with your airs and forget your bodily frame, there might still be some hope for you. Why, you cannot even take care of yourself, how can you take care of the world? Go away and do not interfere with my business.'

Tsekung's countenance changed and he felt ill at ease. He ran for thirty *li* (ten miles) before he recovered himself.

'Who was the fellow you talked with?' asked his disciple. 'Why is it that after meeting him, your face changed and you have not recovered yourself for a whole day?'

'I thought,' said Tsekung, 'there was only one person (Confucius) in this world. I did not know there was another person. I heard from my master that one should try to do things and accomplish things, and that one should try to achieve the greatest results with the greatest economy of labour. That is the teaching of the Sage. But now it seems I am all wrong According to the teaching of (the other) sage, one who embraces the Tao has wholeness of character, from wholeness of character comes wholeness of the body, and from wholeness of the body comes wholeness of the soul. One should live long with other people without knowing where he is going, thus retaining his purity of character. Accomplishments, utility and cunning will cause one to lose one's heart. But this man does not do anything or go anywhere without following the bent of his heart. If the whole world praises him and understands him, he does not care; and if the whole world criticises him and misunderstands him, he still ignores it. Fame and criticism cannot touch him. He is one who has achieved wholeness of character.' (3:12)

57.2. WHY THERE ARE CRIMINALS. Pochu who was a student of Lao Tan (Lao tzu) said to him one day, 'Let's travel and see the world.'

'Why bother? The world is just like this place.'

Pochu insisted again and Lao Tan replied, 'Where do you want to go?'

'Let's go to Ch'i first.'

When they arrived at Ch'i, they saw an (executed) criminal whose body was lying face up on the ground and was covered. Lao Tan took off his formal gown and placed it over his body. He cried to heaven and wept over him, saying, 'You! You! A calamity is coming to the world and you are the first to escape it.'

And Lao Tan continued, 'People say, perhaps he was a thief or perhaps he was a murderer. With the distinctions of honour and disgrace, the fears of mankind appear, and with the accumulation of wealth, struggle for existence appears. Now (the ruler) first sets up what leads to fears, hoards up himself what the people strive to obtain, and makes them labour in poverty without rest. What else can be the result? The ancient rulers gave credit to the people and took the blame on themselves. They always thought the people were right and they themselves wrong. If there was one person deformed, the ruler felt himself responsible. Now it is all different. He keeps the affairs of the country secret from the people and blames them for their ignorance. He sends them on dangerous missions and punishes those who dare not go. He gives them heavy responsibility and punishes those who are unequal to them, and he sends them to a distant place and kills those who do not turn up. When the people are exhausted and cannot cope with the situation, then they have to practice deception. When the ruler daily deceives the people, how can the people help but try to deceive the ruler? For when a man has not the strength to do what he is required to do, then he tries to deceive; when a man cannot cope with a situation, he tries to cover up; and when a man has not enough money to spend, he tries to steal. Upon whom should we place the responsibility for the conduct of the robbers and thieves?' (7:3)

'I do nothing and the people are reformed of themselves.'--*See selection 37.2.*

59. BE SPARING

In managing human affairs, there is no better rule than to be sparing.[6]
To be sparing is to forestall;
To forestall is to be prepared and strengthened;
To be prepared and strengthened is to be ever-victorious;
To be ever-victorious is to have infinite capacity;
He who has infinite capacity is fit to rule a country,
And the Mother (principle) of a ruling country can long endure.
   This is to be firmly rooted, to have deep strength,
   The road to immortality and enduring vision.

6 *Never do too much.*

Probably the saying by Lao tzu which lends itself to interpretation by later followers of the practice of Taoist black art is the last line of Chapter 59. The transition from Lao tzu's mystic union with Nature to direct efforts to become a fairy is perhaps natural. Anyway, in popular religion, Taoist mythology is full of such 'immortals,' and there is not a generation in Chinese history where some Taoist recluses were not reputed to have achieved immortality of this kind. Curiously, Chuang tzu already introduced a number of phrases which are closely allied to the practice, such as 'introspection,' 'mental hygiene', 'nourishing the spirit' and 'breathing through the soul'. etc., terms which are reminiscent of the Indian practice of Yoga. I have arranged here a few selections of Chuang tzu which bear on the cult of immortality.

59.1. 'THE ART OF NOURISHING THE SPIRIT.' There are those who are artificial and abstemious in conduct, strange in manners and live apart from society, who indulge in high-sounding talks and sharp criticism of others, all designed to show one's high mindedness--these are the recluses of the forests. Those who think that society is wrong and are ready to commit suicide by leaping into the sea love such teachings. There are those who occupy themselves with discussions of humanity and justice, loyalty and honesty, respect, humility and courtesy, teachings designed for self-cultivation--these are the social philosophers. The schoolmen and travelling students loved such teachings. Occupied in talks about great service to the country and making a big name, about courtesy between ruler and subjects and order between officials and the people, topics concerned with the administration of the country--these are the courtiers and politicians. Those who wish to help their sovereign make their country become strong and expand and conquer their neighbours' territory by force love such teachings. To go to a lake and live out in the open and fish at leisure for the object of succeeding in doing nothing--these are the scholars of the rivers and seas. Those who wish to retire from the world and enjoy leisure love such doctrines. To control one's breathing, expelling the foul air and inhaling the fresh, to stretch like a bear and crane like a bird for the purpose of achieving a long life--these are the believers of mental hygiene (*taoyin, in practice similar to Yoga*). Those who wish to strengthen their bodies and achieve longevity like P'engtsu love such teachings.

But to be high-minded without artificiality, to cultivate oneself without the teachings of humanity and justice, to believe in governmental order without caring for meritorious service and a high reputation, to have leisure without retiring to the rivers and seas, and to live a long life without the practice of mental hygiene, forgetting nothing, and possessing everything, to be detached and infinitely dispassionate and yet to possess all the virtues--this is the Tao of the universe and the character of the Sage. Therefore it is said mellowness, calm, passivity and inaction[7] represent the state of repose of the universe and the substance of Tao and Teh. Therefore it is said the Sag takes repose. From repose comes unaffected simplicity and from unaffected simplicity comes mellowness. When one is simple and unaffected and mellow, sorrows and fears cannot disturb him and evil influences cannot affect him, thereby one's character becomes whole and his spirit becomes unimpaired. Therefore it is said, the Sage follows nature in his life and goes back to nature at his death. In his quietness he shares the same character with *yin*; in his activity the same energy with *yang*. He responds only when moved, acts only when he is urged, and rises to action only when he is compelled to do so. He regards his life like a floating dream and regards his death as rest. He does not plan, contrive or calculate. He shines but does not dazzle, is honest but does not rely on observing of contracts. Sleeping without dreams, and waking up without worries, his spirit is pure and his soul is never tired.....Therefore it is said, absolute purity of character, unchangeable calm and quiet, mellowness and inaction, and activity in accordance with Nature--these are the ways of nourishing the spirit. (4:8, 9)

7 See the long discussion on these virtues in selection 37.1

59.2. PERFECT TALENT.

'What do you mean by his talents being perfect?' asked the Duke.

'Life and Death,' replied Confucius, 'possession and loss, success and failure, poverty and wealth, virtue and vice, good and evil report, hunger and thirst, heat and cold--these are changes of things in the natural course of events. Day and night they follow upon one another, and no man can say where they spring from. Therefore they must not be allowed to disturb the natural harmony, nor enter into the soul's domain. One should live in a sweet, harmonious atmosphere without being driven to sharpness of temper, and by day and by night share the (peace of) spring with the created things. Thus continuously one creates the seasons in one's own breast. Such a person may be said to have a perfect talent.' (2:3)

59.3. SEE THE SOLITARY ONE. Nanpo Tsek'uei said to Nu Yu(or Female Yu), 'You are of a high age, and yet you have a child's complexion. How is this?'
  Nu Yu replied, 'I have learnt Tao.'
  'Could I get Tao by studying it?' asked the other.

'No! How can you?' said Nu Yu. 'You are not the type of person. There was Puliang I. He had the natural talent of a sage, but did not know the teachings. I knew all the teachings but did not have the natural talent. I wanted to teach him in the hope that he might become a sage. It should have been easy to teach the doctrines of a sage to one who had the natural endowment for them. But it was not so, for I had to wait patiently to reveal it to him. In three days, he could transcend this world. Again I waited for seven days more, then he could transcend all material existence. After he could transcend all material existence, I waited for another nine days, after which he could transcend all life. After he could transcend all life, then he had the clear vision of the morning, and after that, was able to see the Solitary (One). After seeing the Solitary, he could abolish the distinctions of past and present. After abolishing the past and present, he was able to enter there where life and death are no more, where killing does not take away life, nor does giving birth bring life into being. He was ever in accord with his environment, accepting all and welcoming all, regarding everything as destroyed and everything as in completion. This is to be "secure amidst confusion," reaching security through chaos.' (2:6)

59.4. GETTING RID OF MIND AND BODY.

Yen Huei spoke to Chungni (Confucius), 'I am getting on.'
'How so?' asked the latter.
'I have got rid of humanity and justice,' replied the former.
'Very good,' replied Chungni, 'but not quite perfect.'
Another day, Yen Huei met Chungni and said, 'I am getting on.'
'How so?'
'I have got rid of ceremonies and music,' answered YenHuei.
'Very good,' said Chungni, 'but not quite perfect.'
Another day, Yen Huei again met Chungni and said, 'I am getting on.'
'How so?'
'I can forget myself while sitting (in a room),' replied YenHuei.
'What do you mean by that?' said Chungni, changing his countenance.

'I have freed myself from my body,' answered Yen Huei. 'I have discarded my reasoning powers. And by thus getting rid of my body and mind, I have become One with the Infinite. This is what I mean by forgetting myself while sitting.'

'If you have become One,' said Chungni, 'there can be no room for bias. If you have lost yourself, there can be no more hindrance. Perhaps you are really a wise one. I trust to be allowed to follow in your steps.' (2:9)

60. RULING A BIG COUNTRY

Rule a big country as you would fry small fish.[8]
Who rules the world in accord with Tao
    Shall find that the spirits lose their power.
It is not that the spirits lose their power,
    But that they cease to do people harm.
It is not (only) that they cease to do people harm,
    The Sage (himself) also does no harm to the people.
When both do not do each other harm,
    The original character is restored.

8 Let alone, or the fish will become paste by constant turning about.

The first line of the preceding chapter speaks of managing human affairs; the present speaks of ruling a big country. In each case, the idea of exercising restraint and not overdoing a thing is the same. Lao tzu speaks of governmental interference as resulting in harm to the people.

60.1. 'THE SAGE DOES NO HARM TO THE PEOPLE.' The Sage lives with people, but does no harm to the people. Who does no harm to other people cannot be harmed by others. Only he who is beyond harm can go about freely among the people.(6:5)

60.2. 'THE SPIRITS CEASE TO DO PEOPLE HARM.' King Huan was hunting on a lake, with Kuan Chung driving the carriage. The King held Kuan Chung's hand and asked him, 'Did you see anything, Mr Kuan?' ' I didn't see anything,' replied Kuan Chung.

The King returned and fell ill from fight. For several days he did not appear at court. There was a scholar of Ch'i by the name of Huangtse Kao-ao, who said to the King, 'How can ghosts harm you? The harm comes from yourself.'(5:6)

61. BIG AND SMALL COUNTRIES

A big country (should be like) the delta low-regions,
    Being the concourse of the world,
    (And) the Female of the world.
The Female overcomes the Male by quietude,
 And achieves the lowly position by quietude.

Therefore if a big country places itself below a small country,
    It absorbs[9] the small country;
(And) if a small country places itself below a big country,
    It absorbs the big country.
Therefore some place themselves low to absorb (others),
Some are (naturally) low and absorb (others).
    What a big country wants is but to shelter others,
    And what a small country wants is but to be able to come in
        and be sheltered
Thus (considering) that both may have what they want,
    A big country ought to place itself low.

9 *Ch'i, takes, conquers,* overcomes, wins over.

    Chuang tzu never speaks of the Female overcoming the Male. Seethe preface.
'The great sea does not object to flowing eastwards' (or downwards): see 32.1.

62. THE GOOD MAN'S TREASURE

Tao is the mysterious secret of the universe,
The good man's treasure,
And the bad man's refuge.

    Beautiful sayings can be sold at the market,
      Noble conduct can be presented as a gift.
Though there be bad people,
Why reject them?
Therefore on the crowning of an emperor,
    On the appointment of the Three Ministers,
    Rather than send tributes of jade and teams of four horses,
    Send in the tribute of Tao.
Wherein did the ancients prize this Tao?
Did they not say, 'to search for the guilty ones and pardon them?'
Therefore is (Tao) the treasure of the world.

62.1. WHY REJECT PEOPLE?

    'The meanest person in heaven would be the best on earth; and the best on earth would be the meanest person in heaven.' *See selection 33-7.*

    'One who knows the truth about all-sufficiency seeks nothing, loses nothing, and rejects nothing.' *See selection 32. I.*

63. DIFFICULT AND EASY

    Accomplish do-nothing.
    Attend to no-affairs.
    Taste the flavourless.
Whether it is big or small, many of few,
Requite hatred with virtue.
    Deal with the difficult while yet it is easy;
    Deal with the big while yet it is small.
The difficult (problems) of the world
    Must be dealt with while they are yet easy;
The great (problems) of the world
    Must be dealt with while they are yet small.
Therefore the Sage by never dealing with great (problems)
    Accomplishes greatness.

He who lightly makes a promise
    Will find it often hard to keep his faith.

He who makes light of many things
    Will encounter many difficulties.
Hence even the Sage regards things as difficult,
    And for that reason never meets with difficulties.

64. BEGINNING AND END

That which lies still is easy to hold;
    That which is not yet manifest is easy to forestall;
That which is brittle (like ice) easily melts;
    That which is minute easily scatters.
Deal with a thing before it is there;
Check disorder before it is rife.
    A tree with a full span's girth begins from a tiny sprout;
    A nine-storied terrace begins with a clod of earth.
    A journey of a thousand *li* begins at one's feet.

He who acts, spoils;
He who grasps, lets slip.
Because the Sage does not act, he does not spoil,
Because he does not grasp, he does not let slip.
    The affairs of men are often spoiled within an ace of completion,
    By being careful at the end as at the beginning
    Failure is averted.

Therefore the Sage desires to have no desire,
    And values not objects difficult to obtain.
Learns that which is unlearned,
    And restores what the multitude have lost.
That he may assist in the course of Nature
    And not presume to interfere.

63.1. 'REQUITE EVIL WIIH VIRTUE.' To be insulted and not feel angry is the mark of one who had identified himself with the natural scheme of things. (6:10)

64.1. 'BEING CAREFUL AT THE END AS AT THE BEGINNING.' Those who compete in skill begin with *yang* and end up with *yin*, and in overdoing it, the result is useless ornamentation. Those who drink at a formal banquet begin in order and end in disorder, and in overdoing it, the result is intemperate pleasure. This is true of all affairs also. What begins in propriety often ends in impropriety. What begins modestly end up in extravagance. (1:15)

64.2. LEARNING WHAT THE MULTITUDE HAVE LOST. Those who cultivate their abilities in mere worldly studies, hoping thereby to recover their original nature, and those who confuse the desires of their minds in worldly thoughts, hoping thereby to reach enlightenment--these are people seeking in the dark.(4:9)

65. THE GRAND HARMONY

The ancients who knew how to follow the Tao
    Aimed not to enlighten the people,
    But to keep them ignorant.
The reason it is difficult for the people to live in peace
    Is because of too much knowledge.
Those who seek to rule a country by knowledge
    Are the nation's curse.
Those who seek not to rule a country by knowledge
    Are the nation's blessing.
Those who know these two (principles)
    Also know the ancient standard,
And to know always the ancient standard
    Is called the Mystic Virtue.
When the Mystic Virtue becomes clear, far-reaching,
    And things revert back (to their source),
    Then and then only emerges the Grand Harmony.

Few modern readers can be in sympathy with Lao tzu's nihilistic rejection of knowledge and his teaching of 'keeping the people ignorant.' Lao tzu's harking back to the golden age of primitive simplicity (cf. Rousseau) led in this instance to a retrogressive thesis. It should be remembered that the whole Lao tzu philosophy was against over-development of knowledge and learning, and insisted that not only the people should return to primitive simplicity, but the King and the Sage himself also should do so. Furthermore, it was from a period of political world chaos, in which man's intellectual progress showed no commensurate moral advance, that such nihilistic philosophy developed as a protest. The confusion brought by the famous teachers in Chuang tzu's time is described in 65.1. Wars, taxation and conscription had impoverished the people. Famous scholars travelled from country to country to offer their solutions for peace. Idealistic Confucians preached humanity and justice, and realistic politicians offered futile plans for achieving peace. Both types made a great reputation for themselves, and it was the fashion for the rulers of the different countries to make a great deal of fuss about these famous scholars and teachers. Chuang tzu's text makes it clear that the protest was specifically made against the fuss made over such travelling scholars.

65.1. THE ORIGIN OF WORLD CHAOS.

But nowadays anyone can make the people strain their necks and stand on tiptoes by saying, 'In such and such a place there is a Sage.' Immediately they put together a few provisions and hurry off, neglecting their parents at home and their masters' business abroad, going on foot through the territories of the princes, and riding hundreds of miles away. Such is the evil effects of the rulers' desire for knowledge. When the rulers desire knowledge and neglect Tao, the empire is overwhelmed in confusion.

How can this be shown? When the knowledge of bows and cross-bows and hand-nets and tailed arrows increases, then there is confusion among the birds of the air. When the knowledge of hooks and bait and nets and traps increases, then there is confusion among the fishes of the deep. When the knowledge of fences and nets and snares increases, then there is confusion among the beasts of the field. When cunning and deceit and flippancy and the sophistries of the 'hard' and 'white' and identities and differences increase in number and variety, then they overwhelm the world with logic.

Therefore it is that there is often chaos in the world, and the love of knowledge is ever at the bottom of it. For all men strive to grasp what they do not know, while none strive to grasp what they already know; and all strive to discredit what they do not excel in, while none strive to discredit what they do excel in. That is why there is chaos. Thus, above, the splendour of the heavenly bodies is dimmed; below, the power of land and water is burned up, while in between the influence of the four seasons is upset. There is not one tiny worm that moves on earth or an insect that flies in the air but has lost its original nature. Such indeed is the world chaos caused by the desire for knowledge!

Ever since the time of the Three Dynasties downwards, it has been like this. The simple and the guileless have been set aside; the specious and the cunning have been exalted. Tranquil inaction has given place to love of disputation; and disputation alone is enough to bring chaos upon the world. (3:5)

The chaos resulting from the preaching of Confucians and Motseans and the condition of the people may be seen from selection 19.2, which states the same thesis.

65.2. THE HARM DONE TO MAN'S NATURE BY THE 'SAGES.'

Horses live on dry land, eat grass and drink water. When pleased, they rub their necks together. When angry, they turn round and kick up their hoofs at each other. Thus far only do heir natural instincts carry them. But bridled and bitted, with a moon-shaped metal plate on their foreheads, they learn to cast vicious looks, to turn their heads to bite, to nudge at the yoke, to cheat the bit of their mouths or steal the bridle off their heads. Thus their minds and gestures become like those of thieves. This is the fault of Polo (the famous horse-trainer).

In the days of Ho Hsu,[10] the people did nothing in particular at their homes and went nowhere in particular in their walks. Having food, they rejoiced; tapping their bellies, they wandered about. Thus far the natural capacities of the people carried them. The Sages came then to make them bow and bend with ceremonies and music, in order to regulate the external forms of intercourse, and dangled humanity and justice before them.

10 A mythical ruler.

in order to keep their minds in submission. Then the people began to labour and develop a taste for knowledge, and to struggle with one another in their desire for gain, to which here is no end. This is the error of the Sages. (3:3)

65.3. PREDICTION OF CANNIBALISM. THE FUTILITY OF THE CONFUCIAN SOLUTION.

'Besides, to exalt the talented men and give power to the able person, and to offer the highest salaries to the good men are something that was practised long ago by Emperors Yao and Shun....What was there in (the reign of)these two rulers that was worthy of commendation? Such arguments are like cultivating weeds by digging holes in walls, like combing one's hair one by one and cooking rice grain by rain. How can such superficial attention to details help to put the world in order? Exalt the talented men to power and the people begin to plot against each other; give power to the wise and the people begin to deceive one another. Such inducements are not methods by which to benefit the people. For the people's minds are ever in search of profits. Sons will kill their fathers, subjects will murder their rulers. Daylight robbery will be committed and burglars will drill holes through houses in broad daylight. I tell you, the origin of chaos must be found in Emperors Yao and Shun, and its effect will be felt a thousand generations from now, when men will be found to devour one another.' (Says Kengsangch'u) (6.6)

65.4. GOING BACK TO NATURE. PARABLE OF THE SEA BIRD.

Once a sea bird alighted in the suburbs of Lu, and the Duke of Lu brought it home and gave it a welcome dinner at the temple. The *Chiu-shao* music was played by the orchestra and the bird was offered delicacies from the royal sacrifice. The bird stared at all this in sorrow, without tasting one morsel or drinking from one cup, and after three days it died. This is the method of keeping birds by one's own (human) standard, and not by the standard of a bird, by what man imagines the bird likes, and not by what the bird itself likes. To keep a bird by what the bird likes, one should let it loose in a deep forest, let it fly over ponds and islets and float over lakes and rivers. One should feed it with little eels and let it fly or stop where it pleases. How foolish it is to make so much noise with an orchestra when its only fear is human voices? (5:2)

For Chuang tzu's description of the 'Mystic Virtue' and the 'Grand Harmony,' see selection 16.4.

66. THE LORDS OF THE RAVINES

How did the great rivers and seas become the Lords of the
   Ravines?
By being good at keeping low.
That was how they became the Lords of the Ravines.[11]
Therefore in order to be the chief among the people,
   One must speak like their inferiors.
In order to be foremost among the people,
   One must walk behind them.
Thus it is that the Sage stays above,
   And the people do not feel his weight;
Walks in front,
   And the people do not wish him harm.
Then the people of the world are glad to uphold him for ever.
Because he does not contend,
No one in the world can contend against him.

11 Chapters 8 and 66.

66.1. BEING LIKE AN INFERIOR TO PEOPLE
'A distinguished man who can act as other men's inferior is sure to obtain the following of men.' (6:13)

The same idea is treated in Ch. 7.
'The great sea does not object to flowing eastwards' *--see selection 32.1.*

67. THE THREE TREASURES

All the world says: my teaching (Tao) greatly resembles folly.
   Because it is great; therefore it resembles folly.
If it did not resemble folly,
   It would have long ago become petty indeed!

I have Three Treasures;
Guard them and keep them safe;
   The first is Love. [12]
   The second is, Never too much.[13]
   The third is, Never be the first in the world.
Through Love, one has no fear;
Through not doing too much, one has amplitude (of reserve
   power);
Through not presuming to be the first in the world,
   One can develop one's talent and let it mature.
If one forsakes love and fearlessness,
   forsakes restraint and reserve power,
   forsakes following behind and rushes in font,
He is doomed!
For love is victorious in attack,
   And invulnerable in defence.[14]
Heaven arms with love
   Those it would not see destroyed.

12 Ts'e, tender love (associated with the mother).
13 Chien, lit. 'frugality,' 'be sparing'; see Chapter 59.
14 See Chapters 31, 69.

   For this chapter, which contains Lao tzu's most beautiful teachings. Chuang tzu has no parallel passages expressing the same ideas, except for his general counsel of restraint in the form of mellowness and passivity.

68. THE VIRTUE OF NOT-CONTENDING

The brave soldier is not violent;
The good fighter does not lose his temper;
The great conqueror does not fight (on small issues);
The good user of men places himself below others.
-This is the virtue of not-contending,
   Is called the capacity to use men,
   Is reaching to the height of being
      Mated to Heaven, to what was of old.

69. CAMOUFLAGE

There is the maxim of military strategists;
> I dare not be the first to invade, but rather be the invaded.[15]
> Dare not press forward an inch, but rather retreat a foot.

That is, to march without formations,
> To roll not up the sleeves,
> To charge not in frontal attacks,
> To arm without weapons.[16]

There is no greater catastrophe than to underestimate the enemy.
To underestimate the enemy might entail the loss of my treasures.[17]
> Therefore when two equally matched armies meet,
> It is the man of sorrow[18] who wins.

15 Invader and invaded, lit. 'host' and 'guest.' It is possible to read it differently by supplying the often dropped when: 'When I dare not be the invader, then I will be the defender.'
16 Or to feel like being in this condition, i.e., the subjective condition of humility. This is entirely consistent with Lao tzu's philosophy of camouflage, the earliest in the world. Cf. 'great eloquence is like stuttering,' etc., Ch. 45.
17 Possibly the 'Three Treasures' in Ch. 67.
18 Who hates killing. See Ch. 31. The corrected text of Yu Yueh would make this read, 'The man who yields wins.'

The following selection is from a chapter in Chuang tzu which is in all probability spurious. I have included it here both because the subject matter itself is interesting and also because it illustrates the type of thinking already developed in the third and fourth centuries B.C.

68.1. ON NOT FIGHTING.
King T'an Fu (ancestor of the founder of Chou Dynasty) was ruling in Pin. which was under constant attack by the Ti (barbarians).

He offered the enemy hides and silks and dogs and horses and jewels and jade, but the invader would not accept these gifts. It was realised, therefore, that what the Tis wanted was his territory, and King T'an Fu said (to the people of Pin), 'To live with an elder brother and allow his younger brother to be killed, and to live with the father and allow his sons to be killed, this I cannot do. You should all try to remain here. What is the difference between being my subjects and being the subjects of Tis? Besides, I have heard it said that one should not injure the people to be supported on account of the means of support (i.e., on account of the territory).' Then he took a cane and left the country, and the people fell in line and followed him. They thus together founded a new kingdom at the foot of the Chi mountain. Now, such a man like King T'an Fu may be said to be one who valued the people's lives.

Three generations of the kings of Yueh were assassinated, and Prince Sou was worried and ran away to a mountain cave. The people of Yueh were left without a king and they searched for Prince Sou in vain. Finally, they located him at the cave and the Prince refused to come out. The people smoked him out by burning herbs. Then they put him on the royal carriage and when Prince Sou mounted the carriage, he turned his head up and cried. 'To be a king! To be a king! Why don't you people leave me alone?' Prince Sou did not mind being a king; what he minded was the troubles that went with being a king. A person like Prince Sou may be said to be one who would not injure his own life on account of a kingdom. This was exactly the type of king that the people of Yueh wanted.

The States of Han and Wei were fighting for territory. When Tsehuatse went to see Duke Chao Hsi, he found the latter looking dejected, and Tsehuatse said to him, 'Suppose you had an inscription in front of you which read as follows: "Take it with your left hand and your right hand will be paralyzed. Take it with your right hand, and your left hand will be paralyzed." In this case, if by taking it you could have the whole world as your domain, would you take it?'

'No, I would not,' replied Duke Chao Hsi.

'Very well,' said Tsehuatse. 'This seems to show that your two arms are more important than the world. Now your body is certainly more important than your two arms and, on the other hand, the State of Han is far smaller than the world. What you are fighting for is even smaller than the whole State of Han. And yet, you are injuring yourself and sorrowing on account of being unable to get that territory.'

'Good' said the Duke. 'I have many advisers but none gives me this kind of advice.'

Tsehuatse may be said to be a person who knows the relative importance of things. (8:1)

70. THEY KNOW ME NOT

My teachings are very easy to understand and very easy to
    practise,
But no one can understand them and no one can practise them.
    In my words there is a principle.
    In the affairs of men there is a system.
Because they know not these
They also know me not.
    Since there are few that know me,
    Therefore I am distinguished.
Therefore the Sage wears a coarse cloth on top
    And carries jade within his bosom.

71. SICK-MINDEDNESS

Who knows that he does not know is the highest;
Who (pretends to) know what he does not know is sick-minded.
And who recognizes sick-mindedness as sick-mindedness is not sick-minded.
The Sage is not sick-minded.
Because he recognize sick-mindedness as sick-mindedness,
Therefore he is not sick-minded.

'One who does not know really knows, and one who knows really does not know.' *See selection I.1.*
'Do you know that what you consider knowing is really not knowing?' *See selection 56.3.*

72. ON PUNISHMENT (I)

When people have no fear of force,[19]
  Then (as is the common practice) great force descends upon them.

Despise not their dwellings,
Dislike not their progeny.
  Because you do not dislike them,
  You will not be disliked yourself.
Therefore the Sage knows himself, but does not show himself,
  Loves himself, but does not exalt himself.
Therefore he rejects the one (force) and accepts the other(gentility).

19 Wei, military force or authority; sometimes also used in connection with 'God' anger.' Another interpretation, 'when the people have no fear of God, then God'?anger descends upon them.' But this does not fit in so well with the context. See the next two chapters on the futility of punishment, especially the first two lie, Ch. 74

73. ON PUNISHMENT (2)

Who is brave in daring (you) kill,
Who is brave in not daring (you) let live.

In these two,
  There is some advantage and some disadvantage.
  (Even if) Heaven dislikes certain people,
  Who would know (who are to be killed and) why?
Therefore even the Sage regards it as a difficult question.
  Heaven's Way (Tao) is good at conquest without strife,
  Rewarding (vice and virtue) without words,

Making its appearance without call,
   Achieving results without obvious design.
The heaven's net is broad and wide.[20]
With big meshes, yet letting nothing slip through.

> 20 This has now become a Chinese proverb for 'virtue always rewarded, vice always punished.'

74. ON PUNISHMENT (3)

The people are not afraid of death;
Why threaten them with death?
   Supposing that the people are afraid of death,
   And we can seize and kill the unruly,
   Who would dare to do so?[21]
Often it happens that the executioner is killed.
And to take the place of the executioner
   Is like handling the hatchet for the master carpenter.
He who handles the hatchet for the master carpenter
   Seldom escapes injury to his hands.

21 Notice the similarity of construction with the first five lines of Ch. 73.

   The Chapters 72, 73, 74 contain Lao tzu's important statements on crime and punishment.
   On the origin of criminals, see selection 57.2

   'From the three dynasties downwards, the world has lived in a helter-skelter of promotions and punishments. What chance have the people left for fulfilling peacefully the natural instincts of their lives?' *See selection. 3.4.*
   'Henceforth, man's character declines and punishments are instituted.' *See selection 17.2.*

75. ON PUNISHMENT (4)

When people are hungry,
It is because their rulers eat too much tax-grain.

Therefore the unruliness of hungry people
   Is due to the interference of their rulers.
   That is why they are unruly.
The people are not afraid of death,
Because they are anxious to make a living.
That is why they are not afraid of death.
   It is those who interfere not with their living
   That are wise in exalting life.

'For it is not difficult to get the people to live peacefully with one another.' *See selection 17.1.*

75.1. ON VALUING LIFE. Prince Mou of Chungshan said to Chantse, 'I am living at present abroad. But my mind keeps thinking of my palace at Wei. What should I do?'
   'Think of your life first,' replied Chantse, 'for if you value your life, then you put less weight on the luxuries of life.' (8:3)

BOOK SEVEN

APHORISMS

76. HARD AND SOFT

When man is born, he is tender and weak;
   At death, he is hard and stiff.
When the things and plants are alive, they are soft and supple;
When they are dead, they are brittle and dry.
   Therefore hardness and stiffness are the companions of death,
   And softness and gentleness are the companions of life.
Therefore when an army is headstrong[1], it will lose in battle.
When a tree is hard, it will be cut down.
   The big and strong belong underneath.
   The gentle and weak belong at the top.[2]

1 *Ch'iang means 'stiff,' 'strong,' and 'headstrong.'*
2 *As with twigs and trunks.*

77. BENDING THE BOW

The Tao (way) of Heaven,
Is it not like the bending of a bow?
    The top comes down and the bottom-end goes up,
    The extra (length) is shortened, the insufficient (width) is
      expanded.
It is the Way of Heaven to take away from those that have too
  much
And give to those that have not enough.
Not so with man's way:
    He takes away from those that have not
    And gives it as tribute to those that have too much.
Who can have enough and to spare to give to the entire world?
Only the man of Tao.
Therefore the Sage acts, but does not possess,
    Accomplishes but lays claim to no credit,
    Because he has no wish to seem superior.

78. NOTHING WEAKER THAN WATER

There is nothing weaker than water
But none is superior to it in overcoming the hard,
For which there is no substitute.
    That weakness overcomes strength
    And gentleness overcomes rigidity,
    No one does not know;
    No one can put into practice.

Therefore the Sage says:
    'Who receives unto himself the calumny of the world
    Is the preserver of the state.
    Who bears himself the sins of the world
    Is the king of the world.'
Straight words seem crooked.

On the danger of relying on an army, see selection 30.1.

77.I. TO HAVE ENOUGH IS GOOD LUCK. To have enough is good luck, to have more than enough is harmful. This is true of all things but especially of money. (8:8)

The selection is from a spurious chapter.
On weakness overcoming strength. See selection 14.4.
The line, 'Who receives unto himself the calumny of the world is the preserver of the state,' *is given in the Prolegomena as one of the basic teachings of Lao tzu.*

79. PEACE SETTLEMENTS

Patching up a great hatred is sure to leave some hatred behind.
How can this be regarded as satisfactory?
Therefore the Sage holds the left tally,[3]
And does not put the guilt on the other party.
The virtuous man is for patching up;
The vicious is for fixing guilt. [4]
But 'the way of Heaven is impartial;
It sides only with the good man.'[5]

[3] *Sign of inferiority in an agreement.*
[4] *Wang Pi's commentary: 'for pointing out faults.' This in modern days is embodied in the 'guilt cause,' which is always determined by the victor in the battle.*
[5] *An ancient quotation appearing in many ancient texts.*

79.1. ON THE FUTILITY OF TREATIES. To make a peace settlement which is not peaceful (unjust) will result only in an unpeaceful peace. To pledge faith with the faithless will result only in a faithless pledge. The clever people become lost in their own devices, while the divine man can go straight to the truth. It has long been established that the clever people cannot pitch themselves against the spiritual man, but the fools stick to their prejudices and are submerged in the events of the day.(As a result), all their accomplishments concern the external details. Is this not sad indeed? (8:15)

79.2. THE SON OF HEAVEN. Whom the people follow may be called the people of Heaven. Whom Heaven assists is called the son of Heaven. (6:7)

80. THE SMALL UTOPIA

(Let there be) a small country with a small population,
Where the supply of goods are tenfold or hundredfold, more
    than they can use.
Let the people value their lives[6] and not migrate far.
   Though there be boats and carriages,
    None be there to ride them.
   Though there be armour and weapons,
    No occasion to display them.
Let the people again tie ropes for reckoning,
   Let them enjoy their food,
   Beautify their clothing,
   Be satisfied with their homes,
   Delight in their customs.
The neighbouring settlements overlook one another
So that they can hear the barking of dogs and crowing of cocks of
    their neighbors,
And the people till the end of their days shall never have been
    outside their country.

6 Lit. 'death.'

80.1. THE AGE OF PERFECT CHARACTER.
Have you never heard of the Age of Perfect Character? In the days of Yungch'eng, Tat'ing, Pohuang, Chungyang, Lilu, Lihsu, Hsienyuan, Hohsu, Tsunlu, Chuyung, Fuhsi, and Shen nung, the people tied knots for reckoning. They enjoyed their food, beautified their clothing, were satisfied with their homes, and delighted in their customs. Neighbouring settlements over looked one another, so that they could hear the barking of dogs and crowing of cocks of their neighbors, and the people still the end of their days had never been outside their own country. In those days, there was indeed perfect peace. (3:5)

81. THE WAY OF HEAVEN

True words are not fine-sounding;
    Fine-sounding words are not true.
A good man does not argue;
    He who argues is not a good man.
The wise one does not know many things;
    He who knows many things is not wise.

The Sage does not accumulate (for himself):
    He lives for other people,
    And grows richer himself;
    He gives to other people,
    And has greater abundance.

The Tao of Heaven
    Blesses, but does not harm.
The Way of the Sage
    Accomplishes, but does not contend.

81.1. 'TRUE WORDS ARE NOT FINE-SOUNDING.' 'A dog is not considered good because of his barking , and a man is not considered clever because of his ability to talk.' *See selection 32.1.*

'The learned is not necessarily wise, and the good talker is not necessarily clever.' *See selection 4.1.*

81.2. 'HE GIVES TO OTHER PEOPLE.' (The pure man's) spirit goes through high mountains without hindrance and through a deep spring without getting wet, and he lives on low grounds without getting sick. His spirit fills the whole universe. He gives to other people, and has greater abundance. (5:15)

81.3. WHERE CAN I FIND A MAN WHO FORGETS ABOUT WORDS? A bait is used to catch fish. When you have caught the fish, you can forget about the bait. A rabbit trap is used to catch rabbits. When the rabbits are caught, you can forget about the trap. Words are used to express meaning, when you understand the meaning, you can forget about the words. Where can I find a man who forgets about words to talk with him? (7:8)

There are some things that you can talk about, and some things that you appreciate with your heart. The more you talk, the further away you get from the meaning. (7:5)

IMAGINARY CONVERSATIONS BETWEEN LAO TZU AND CONFUCIUS

By Chuang tzu

Chuang tzu fictionised. He said of his own works that nine-tenths were allegories. His way of expounding a philosophical idea was often to select a few characters, historical, legendary or outright fictitious, and let them talk, and his works abound with conversations that were never intended as literal records. This is clear enough from such stories of conversations between General Clouds and The Great Nebulous, between Light and Ether, between the Yellow Emperor, Do-Nothing and No-Beginning, and the dialogues of persons like 'Muddle-head No-such-person,' 'No-toes Shushan,' etc,. etc. The conversations between Lao tzu and Confucius which he wrote must therefore be taken as frankly imaginary, although they sometimes contain references to historical facts in the life of the two philosophers. By common tradition, Lao tzu was the older man and Confucius saw him in his lifetime. Naturally, in these stories by the Taoist philosopher, Confucius was always pictured as receiving advice rather than giving it.

Confucius appears forty or fifty times in different conversations in Chuang tzu's works, and sometimes Confucius's disciples, especially Yen Huei and Tsekung, had encounters with Taoist sages. There are eight imaginary conversations between Confucius and Lao tzu himself, of which one already has been given in selection 4.1.

I

Confucius was going west to give his books to the Chou Imperial Archives. And Tselu thought and said to him, 'I have heard that there is a keeper of the archives at (the capital) Chou. His name is Lao Tan. He has retired and is living at his home. If you want to entrust your books for safe-keeping, why don't you go and give them to him?'

'Good,' said Confucius.

So Confucius went to see Lao Tan and Lao Tan would not accept the books. Confucius spread the Twelve Classic[1] before him, and tried to explain what he had done. Before Confucius had finished, Lao Tan interrupted him, saying, 'You are trying to cover too much material. Tell me the essence of your ideas.'

'The essence is in the teachings of humanity and justice,' said Confucius.

'May I ask, are humanity and justice a part of the nature of man?'

'Yes,' replied Confucius. 'A gentleman's character is not complete without the principle of humanity, and his life is not correct if he does not follow the principle of justice. Humanity and justice are truly a part of the nature of man. What else can they be?'

'May I ask what you mean by humanity and justice?' said Lao Tan.

'To share the happiness with others and to love all mankind without partiality-this is the essence of humanity and justice.'

'Alas!' replied Lao Tan. 'You talk like the latter-day prophets. Isn't it abstruse to talk of love for all mankind? Impartiality implies the recognition of partiality (for individuals). If you want the world to find again its lost shepherd, remember that there is already a constant law governing heaven and earth, the sun and the moon are shining in the sky, the constellations are in their proper places, and the fowl of the air and the beasts of the earth already thrive in flocks and herds, and trees already grow and prosper. Why don't you just follow the natural bent of your character and the laws of Tao? Why do you create

---

1 In the time of Confucius and Chuang tzu, reference was usually made to the 'Six Classics.' There are different interpretations of the meaning of the 'Twelve Classics.'

---

such a commotion, holding the banner of humanity and justice like one who has lost his son and is beating a drum to look for him? Alas! I am afraid you are disturbing the nature of man.'(4:3)

II

Confucius was already fifty-one years old and had not yet heard of Tao. Then he went south to P'ei[2] to sec Lao Tan, and Lao Tan said to him, 'I hear you are a wise man from the north. Have you found the truth (Tao)?'

'Not yet,' replied Confucius.

'How did you go about to search for it?' asked Lao Tan.

'I had been searching for it by a study of government systems and institutions for five years and without avail.'

'Then, what did you do to find the truth?'

'I tried to find it in the principles of *yin* and *yang* for twelve years and again in vain.'

'Yes, you are right,' said Lao Tan. 'For if Tao could be given as a gift, everybody would have offered it as tribute to his ruler. If Tao could be made a present, everybody would have presented it to his parents. If Tao could be told about, everybody would have spoken to his brothers about it. If Tao could be inherited, everybody would have bequeathed it to his children and grandchildren. But no one could do it. Why? Because if you haven't got it in you, you could not receive Tao. If the other person hasn't got it, the truth would not penetrate to him. What is felt in oneself cannot be received from the outside and the sage does not try to communicate it. What is received from the outside cannot stop within, and the sage does not try to keep it. Remember that reputation is something that belongs to the public and should not be striven for too eagerly. Humanity and justice are but like roadside inns to the ancient kings, where one could stop overnight, but not stay permanently. To be seen often is to be criticized often. The perfect men of ancient times

2 Said to be Lao tzu's home town.

travelled by the road of humanity, stopping for a night at the inn of justice, to go on and wander about in the wilds of freedom. They fed themselves by growing food in the field of Without-care and lived in the vegetable garden of No obligations. Freedom means doing nothing: Without-care means there is no problem of food; and No-obligations means there are no expenditures. The ancients called this wandering in search of grace. For a successful man cannot give another person his salary, a famous man cannot donate his fame to others, and a man in a high position cannot give his power to another. Holding that power, a man is frightened when he has it and worried lest he should lose it. And these people go on for ever without ever stopping to see what it is all about. These are the damned by God. Resentment, favour, give, take, censure, advice, life and death--these eight are means for correcting a man's character, but only one who comprehends the great process of this fluid universe without being submerged in it knows how to handle them. Therefore, it is said, "You rectify what can be rectified."When a man's heart cannot see this, the door of his divine intelligence is shut.' (4:6)

III
Confucius saw Lao Tan and talked with him about humanity and justice. And Lao Tan said:

'When one throws dust in your eyes, you lose all sense of direction. When mosquitoes bite you, you cannot sleep all night. This humanity and justice are irritating. They upset my consciousness and cause confusion of mind. If you will allow the people to go on living without loss of their original simplicity, and you yourself will just follow your natural impulses, people's character will be established. Why do you go about impatiently like a man who has lost his son and is beating a drum to look for him? The swan is white without a daily bath and the raven is black without black paint. In their original state, black and white are quite in place. All this seeking after reputation and fame adds nothing to a man's character. When a pool dries up, and fish are left on land, they moisten each other with the foam from their mouth. It would be a much better way to let them back into the rivers and lakes.' (4:7)

IV

'I have studied the Six Classics, the Book of Poetry, the Book of History, the Book of Rites, the Book of Music, the Philosophy of Mutations and the Spring and Autumn Annals,' said Confucius to Lao Tan. 'I think I have studied them for a long time and know them very well. But I have gone around the seventy-two kingdoms to interview their rulers and spoken to them about the principles of government of the ancient kings and the historical records of Dukes Chou and Shao. Not a single one of them wanted to listen to me. Indeed it is so difficult for a man to convince others and for people to understand the truth.'

'Fortunately for you,' replied Lao Tan, 'you did not meet one of those rulers who want to put the world in order. The Six Classics that you speak of are but like footprints left by the ancient kings, and not the persons from whom the footprints come. What you talk about is nothing but such footprints. A footprint is made by a shoe, but it is not the shoe itself. The (male and female) white hawks reproduce their kind by looking at each other without turning their eyes. A male insect chirps in one place and a female insect echoes his cry somewhere below and they reproduce. Certain animals are hermaphrodites and they reproduce by themselves. Each one's nature cannot be changed. Each one's destiny cannot be altered. Time cannot be stopped, and Tao must not be blocked up. With possession of the Tao, one can go wherever one likes. Without the Tao, one is lost wherever one goes.'

Confucius returned and did not stir from his house for three months, after which period he went again to see Lao Tan and said, 'Now I've got it. The birds reproduce by laying eggs, the fish by blowing bubbles, and insects like bees by metamorphosis (from the chrysalis). The elder brother cries when his younger brother is born (in the case of breast-feeding babies). For a long time I have not lost myself in the common humanity, and without losing oneself in the common humanity, how can I teach humanity?'

'Now you've got it,' said Lo Tan. (4:8)

V

Confucius went to see Lao Tan and the latter had just come out of a bath. He was spreading his hair to dry and he looked lifeless as a corpse. Confucius stood aside waiting for him. After a while he said, 'Are my eyes deceiving me, or is it true? Just now, Master, you looked like the dry stump of a tree, standing there alone, like a thing from which the spirit has departed.'

'I was meditating on the origin of the universe.'

'What do you mean?' said Confucius.

'It is a problem that defies the mind and language. I'll try to tell you what it is like approximately. The great *yin* is majestically silent; the great *yang* is impressively active. Majestic silence comes from heaven, and impressive activity comes from the earth. When the two meet and merge, all things are formed Some can see the connection, but cannot see their form. Growth alternates with decay, fullness with exhaustion, darkness with light. Every day things change and every month they are transformed. You see what is going on every day and observe that the change is imperceptible. Life comes from a source and death is but a return to it. Thus beginning follows the end in a continual endless cycle. Without Tao, what can be the generative principle binding on all?'

'May I share in your spiritual wanderings?' asked Confucius.

'One who attains Tao sees perfect beauty and feels perfect happiness,' replied Lao Tan. 'To see perfect beauty and feel perfect happiness is left for the perfect one.'

'Can you speak more in detail?' asked Confucius.

And Lao Tan replied, 'The vegetarian animals do not mind changing their feeding ground. Insects that live in water do not mind change of water. That is because the changes are minor and do not affect their vital needs. Happiness and anger, joys and sorrows, should not enter one's breast, for this universe represents the unity of all things. When one perceives this unity and is united with it, he regards his bodily form as dust of the earth, and the cycle of life and death but as the alternation of day and night. He cannot be disturbed by such accidents, much less by the occurrences of fortune and misfortune. He shakes off an official position as he shakes off dirt, knowing that his self is more precious than rank. His aim is to keep his self without allowing it to become lost in external changes. For the process of change going on in all things is continuous and endless. Why should one let one's mind be troubled by it? One who knows Tao will understand this.'

'Master, your character is comparable to the heaven and earth,' said Confucius, 'and yet even you depend on words of wisdom to cultivate your heart. What ancient men could do without such (self-cultivation)?'

'You're wrong there,' said Lao Tan. 'Look at the water coming out of a spring, it flows naturally of itself. The perfect man does not have to cultivate his character and yet he never departs from the laws of nature. It is like the sky which is high by nature, like the earth which is solid by nature and like the sun and the moon which are bright by themselves. What do they do to cultivate themselves?'

Confucius left and said to Yen Huei, 'In the matter of Tao I am just like a gnat. If the Master had not enlightened my darkness, I would not be aware of the great scheme of the universe.(5:13)

VI

'There are philosophers who discuss different methods of government like chasing one another,' said Confucius to Lao Tan. 'They talk of the true and the false, of possibility and impossibility. The sophists say, "You can analyse (the qualities of) hardness and whiteness as if you could hang them in a corner." Do you think these people can be regarded as sages?'

'They are just good clerks and specialists who worry their minds and their bodily frames about nothing,' replied Lao Tan. 'A good hound is held in leash because he can worry foxes, and a monkey is captured from the hills because of his agility. Come here, Ch'iu, I want to tell you something which you cannot hear and transmit to you something which words cannot express. Many are the people who have a head and toes, but are deficient in hearing and in understanding. There are none who can understand that both the formless and the formed exist, and that movement is the same as rest, death is the same as life, and decline is the same as rise. These are (appearances)which do not go to the bottom of all things. Understanding the principles of order depends on the person himself. To forget the material things and forget one's own nature is to forget one's self. A man who can forget his own self may be said to have entered the realm of Heaven.' (3:12)

VII

Confucius saw Lao Tan and on his return kept quiet for three days.

'Master, when you saw Lao Tan, what kind of advice did you give him?' asked his disciples 'Give him advice?' replied Confucius. 'For the first time I saw a dragon. When the dragon's spirit converges, you see its form, and when it disperses it gives off a radiance of beauty, riding upon the clouds and feeding upon the *yin* and the *yang*. When I saw him I was aghast and could not close my mouth.'

'Is is true, then,' said Tsekung, 'that there are such people who, according to reports, "can sit still like a corpse or spring into action like a dragon, be silent as the deep or talk with the voice of thunder," people who spring into action like (the forces of) the universe? Do you think I can go and see him?'

With an introduction from Confucius, Tsekung went to see Lao Tan. The latter was sitting in his parlour and said with a thin voice, 'I am now getting old. Do you have some advice for me?'

'The Three Kings and Five Emperors ruled the world in different ways, but all of them left a great name for themselves, said Tsekung. 'Why do you consider that they are not sages?'

'Come forward, young man,' said Lao Tan. 'What do you mean when you say they ruled the world in different ways?'

'Emperor Yao gave his throne to Shun and Shun gave his throne to Yu,' replied Tsekung. 'Emperor Yu devoted his labour (to water conservation), and Emperor T'ang devoted his energy to wars. King Wen continued to serve his ruler, Chou, but (his son) King Wu raised the banner of rebellion. That is why I say they employed different methods to rule the world.'

'Come forward, young man,' said Lao Tan. 'I will tell you about the governments of the Three Kings and Five Emperors. In the government under the Yellow Emperor, he encouraged simplicity of heart among his people. Some of his people did not weep when their parents died and it was not considered wrong. In the government under Emperor Yao, he encouraged affection among relatives. Some of his people killed the murderers of their parents, and it was not considered wrong. In the government under Emperor Shun, he encouraged competition. Babies were born after ten months of pregnancy,[3] and an infant learned to talk in five months. Before he was already three years old,

[3] *According to an ancient commentator, human pregnancy used to last fourteen months, and a child learned to talk when he was two years old.*

he could already learn to distinguish persons, and early death came to this world. In the government under Emperor Wu, he changed men's hearts, and men began to have cunning in their hearts and armies were sent out to fight for some good cause. It was not considered wrong to kill 'robbers' (enemies). Then race distinctions arose and each race considered itself living in a complete world by itself. Hence the world was thrown into great confusion and the Confucians and Motseans arose. At first, the discussion was around principles, but now they degenerate into womanish gossip. What can I say? I tell you, people speak of the Three Kings and Five Emperors "ruling" the world, but in actuality they misruled. The knowledge that came with the Three Kings was contrary to the influence of the sun and the moon above, destructive of the energy of land and water below, and subversive to the operation of the seasonal forces in between. That knowledge is more poisonous than a scorpion's tail, than the animal *hsien-kuei*.[4]

Henceforth the people are not able to fulfil peacefully the natural instincts of their lives. And yet these people regard themselves as sages. What a lack of shame!'

Tsekung stood there listening and felt ill at ease. (4:7)

[4] *No commentator can make out what animal is referred to.*

[For the book of **'Chuang tzu'** write by Lin Yutang, you can search on Amazon or buy from book shop.]

Made in the USA
Coppell, TX
25 June 2021